The Sephardic Kosher Kitchen

The Sephardic Kosher Kitchen

by

Suzy David

Illustrations: Jean David

jD | JONATHAN DAVID PUBLISHERS, INC.
MIDDLE VILLAGE, NY 11379

THE SEPHARDIC KOSHER KITCHEN
by Suzy David

Copyright © Keter Publishing House Jerusalem Ltd.

English language copyright, © 1984, Jonathan David Publishers, Inc.
68–22 Eliot Avenue, Middle Village, NY 11379

Jonathan David Publishers, Inc.
68–22 Eliot Avenue
Middle Village, New York 11379

Library of Congress Cataloging in Publication Data

David, Suzy
The Sephardic kosher kitchen.

Translation of: Ha-Mitbah Ha-Sefaradi.
1. Cookery, Jewish   I. Title.

TX724.D3813   1984   641.5'676   84-8150
ISBN 0-8246-0303-6

Printed in Israel by Keterpress Enterprises Ltd., Jerusalem

Contents:

Introduction

My childhood memories are rich with mouth-watering flavors, aromas and foods that recall an entire world.

I was born into the warm surroundings of a closely knit family: my father, a wise, deep-rooted man; my mother, a lavish and perennial giver; and myself, a willful and mischievous only child. We lived on the top floor of a comfortable, old-fashioned, three-story house, whose other floors were occupied by my maternal grandparents and two uncles and their families. In the back there was a wide yard where, after school, I played with my cousins, who, being younger than myself, were rarely spared my bossy attentions; and where in the summer and fall the maids boiled sweets, jams and marmalades over a large open fire — we children eating ourselves sick on the luscious fruit.

Growing up in Sophia, the modest but stately capital of Bulgaria, was an extremely pleasant experience, or so it seems to me now. Bulgaria, to refresh your memory, is one of the small countries of the Balkans, located south of the Danube, on the shores of the Black Sea, and bordered by Yugoslavia, Turkey, Greece and Rumania. Sophia is beautifully situated in a green valley enclosed by rugged mountains, abounding in the rivers and streams that provided us with a dazzling variety of freshwater fish. At the center of the city was the royal palace and close by a wide promenade lined on both sides with magnificent wild chestnut trees. On fine days I strolled there with girlfriends or a very special boyfriend, watching the trees take on a new appearance as the seasons changed, my favorite being the rich reds browns and golds of autumn.

The Jewish community of Bulgaria proudly boasted roots more ancient than the Bulgars themselves, going back at least as far as 70 A.D., probably even before the destruction of the Second Temple, and forming a living link between Europe and Asia. Most of the Jews, though, arrived after the Spanish Inquisition, at the end of the 15th century, when they were faced with the terrible choice of either converting to Christianity or leaving the country in which they had lived for nearly a thousand years.

In Spain the Jews had attained a position of power and prominence. They became personal doctors and counselors to kings and princes, diplomatic emissaries, teachers of philosophy, poets and scholars who wrote in Hebrew, Arabic, Greek and Latin, as well as Spanish Castilian. They constructed synagogues and theological seminaries, and helped to establish flourishing banking institutions and international trade connections. When they arrived in Bulgaria they were welcomed by the Ottoman Turks, who had conquered the land and opened up their empire to the Jewish

7

refugees of Spain and Portugal. Though they never quite regained their former hegemony, the large Jewish communities of the Balkans flourished both culturally and economically.

In S   ia where more than half the country's 45,000 Jews lived, they form   1 a cohesive and prosperous community, which had created for itself a rea uringly measured and seemingly settled way of life. Every morning the men went out to work, largely in commerce, industry and the free professions, while the women kept house with a staff of servants and in the afternoons paid decorous visits to their friends. On the occasions when I ccon panied my mother, I used to sit in the spacious living room, my eyes glued to the door from which a maid would eventually emerge carrying a finely crafted silver platter bearing the little cut-glass containers of *dolces*, as we called the fruits cooked to a confiture in heavy syrup. What a joy!

On the Sabbath and on holidays, the men attended the central Sephardic synagogue, whose simplicity of line recalled in the twentieth century the Islamic influence of former days. We children used to gather in the court-yard, and on Yom Kippur those of us who were old enough to fast carried along a quince studded with cloves to keep us from fainting — or so we thought. Passover and Rosh Hashanah (New Year) were special treats, when the children, who were ordinarily tucked into bed quite early, were allowed to stay up with the grown-ups gathered 50 or so around the festive dinner table laid with a white lace cloth and our best china. They are occasions that now in Israel I look back on wistfully and somewhat sadly.

But what exactly is this cuisine you're about to embark on? It is called *Sephardic* cooking, *Sephard* being the Hebrew word for the Iberian Penin-sula and referring, too, to the Jews who migrated from there. When the Spanish Jews were expelled, they took with them not only their high culture and erudition, but their centuries-old culinary skills and Mediterranean palates. In the course of time their cooking was inevitably modified by the ingredients available locally, changed to incorporate new fruits and vegeta-bles, meats, fish, condiments and spices, and even altered to accommodate different customs. So there are as many types of Sephardic cooking as countries in which Spanish Jews found asylum.

Through the marriage of Balkan and Mediterranean flavors, our Sephardic cuisine acquired its unique character. There are the eggplants, tomatoes and bright red and green peppers of the Spanish Jews as well as the beans and salty white goat's cheese of the Balkans. There is the tender taste of fowl pan-roasted in its own juices, fish served in its own jelly, meat cooked with an infinite variety of vegetables, and an array of vegetable and cheese pies with or without crusts. There are savory foods fried or sautéed in oil and gently spiced with garlic, onion and fresh dill and parsley; and desserts carrying a romantic tinge of attar of roses.

8

Of course what I really mean by Sephardic cooking is my grandmother's. I can still see her clearly, tiny in her immense kitchen, working at a huge, tiled, coal-fed stove to which later was added an electric one, an innovation lacking in dignity. The gigantic copper pots and *pailas* (large, shallow copper pans with two handles) in which the marmalade and confiture were prepared, the jars upon jars of winter preserves, the pantry with its hidden treasures, the cellar filled to the brim with pickled stuffed green peppers, pears and whole heads of cabbage are all part of my childhood recollections.

Grandma was a wonderful cook. She had one rule: whatever she didn't like was no good for the rest of us. Luckily, she liked a great many good things. Every day our family gathered around a formally set table for two three-course meals. Sometimes dairy dishes were served in the evening and fresh fruit instead of cake for desert; Saturday meals tended to be more elaborate, usually starting with fish or brains with an *agristada* (boiled mayonnaise), followed by chicken with rice and peas, and climaxed by fruit or a scrumptious sweet. But all of our meals had the authentic savor of true Sephardic cooking: the most satisfying results achieved by the least complicated means.

Life in Sophia seemed a continuous anticipation of feasts and holidays: the kitchen bursting with excitement, grandmother at the helm preparing the complicated, traditional dishes (i.e., baklava), mother the modern introductions (i.e., torte), the maids rushing about and me tasting whatever I could lay my hands on. I was a great taster, and the tastes lingered.

It was the search for these distant tastes that, in later years, brought me to my kitchen in Israel. I had left Bulgaria in 1943, amidst the calamities of World War II, with scanty luggage that didn't include culinary know-how but did contain a wealth of memories. Later when cooking was no longer a secret language, I tended to return to the flavors of my youth, which evoke for me the harmonious tenor of a lost lifestyle. Unfortunately, by then my mother and grandmother were no longer here to instruct me, so I started to question my aunts, my cousins, my friends and even strangers from the old country. Recipes were tried, compared, kept or discarded. I found out that some things were not as good as I had imagined, while others were more subtle and refined. Since I had no written recipes, gradually — by instinct more than anything else — I put my own order into a vast culinary heritage, which is how this Sephardic cookbook came to be written.

I have decided to emphasize our daily fare, with a sprinkling of holiday dishes. All of the recipes are in keeping with the Jewish dietary laws. Meat and milk ar neither cooked nor served together (though in non-Orthodox families the ubiquitous yoghurt accompanied many meals). I have, however, modified some of the basic recipes by cutting the cooking time of vegetables so as to preserve their texture and vitamins and by reducing the fat content of dishes using oil — with no loss to the original taste.

FIRST COURSES

First Courses

Perhaps our ancestors had sturdier stomachs than we. All of the recipes in this section are for what the title says: full courses — not mere appetizers to whet the taste buds. In fact, there were no little appetizers for us in Bulgaria. Both our midday and evening meals were three-course affairs. Today, each and every one of the recipes in this section can be served up separately as a meal in itself.

Most often, our first course consisted of sweet and sour vegetables. They were usually cooked in a small amount of water to which oil, lemon juice, sugar, salt and pepper were added. We ate them at room temperature, though for a full meal they are better hot.

Brains were another favorite, especially calves' brains, the most delicate of the various types. As they are somewhat perishable, my mother always made sure to buy them fresh and to prepare them on the same day. And for the most appetizing results, she cleaned them with a hawklike thoroughness.

On Sabbaths and holidays, fish usually introduced our meals. Bordering the Black Sea, Bulgaria was ideally situated for a plentiful supply of saltwater fish, while a large selection of freshwater varieties was amply provided by the country's many lakes and rivers. Though each type of fish naturally has its own distinctive flavor, substitutions usually work out quite well, sometimes very interestingly, and I have generally given alternatives.

There are two other types of recipes that I want to account for. One is for soup — a cool and refreshing yoghurt soup for summer and a rich and hearty calves' foot soup for winter. These, in my opinion, typify Sephardic soups. The other is for *agristada*, or a boiled mayonnaise, which can be served by itself or as a tangy addition to brains, fish and chicken cutlets.

Fish Roe Caviar
(Tarama)

Usually served as an hors d'oeuvres or appetizer, this salad is best when made with fresh carp roe; but canned roe, available in specialty food shops, also gives excellent results. It goes well with a stiff drink, especially Pernod or Arak.

1 slice stale white bread, crust removed
1 medium-sized potato, peeled, quartered and cooked until soft
4 ounces carp (or shad) roe, available in Greek and Balkan specialty shops

1 cup light vegetable oil
juice of 1½ lemons
¼ cup soda water (seltzer)
1 medium-sized Spanish onion, chopped finely (to accompany the salad)

Soak the bread in water until it is soft. Squeeze out the excess water and crumble the bread into the bowl of an electric mixer. Add the potato.

Wash the fish roe through a strainer to remove some of the salt. Add the fish roe to the bread and potato and mix together with a fork. Attach bowl to mixer and turn on to slow. Add the oil slowly, as you would for a mayonnaise. When half the oil has been amalgamated, add the lemon juice. Continue to blend in the oil until a mayonnaise-like consistency has been reached. Remove to a storage bowl and blend in the soda water. Store in the refrigerator until ready to serve. The caviar will keep up to a week. Serve in a bowl, with chopped onion over the top, or on the side, with toasted mideastern flat breat (pitta) or wedges of toast.

Serves 6 as first course, more as cocktail accompaniment.

Celeriac in Lemon Sauce
(Apiu Ilado)

Though better known as a soup flavorer, celeriac makes a delicate winter appetizer. The carrots add taste and accent the roots' light yellow color for a lovely, eye-pleasing opener.

2 celeriacs (round celery root)	2 tablespoons olive oil
juice of 2 lemons	1 teaspoon salt
bowl of cold water	10 peppercorns
2 large carrots	pinch of sugar
1 cup water	1 teaspoon coriander seeds

Wash, peel and slice the celery root into rounds of ½ inch thickness. Place them immediately in a bowl of cold water acidulated with the juice of one lemon until ready to cook.

Wash, scrape and slice the carrots thinly.

Drain the celery root, and put it into a saucepan with the carrot slices. Add the cup of water, oil, juice of the remaining lemon, salt, peppercorns, sugar and coriander seeds. Bring to a boil, lower the flame, cover, and simmer until vegetables are soft (about 10–15 minutes). Remove the vegetables to a serving dish. Strain the sauce, return it to the pan, and reduce the liquid by half.

Pour the sauce over the carrots and celery and chill before serving.

Serves 6–8, depending on the size of the celeriac.

Zucchini in Lemon Sauce
(Anginara)

Zucchini was a summer staple in our home. The lemon sauce brings out the vegetable's fresh garden taste.

2 pounds small zucchini	10 peppercorns
½ cup water	1 teaspoon coriander seeds
3 tablespoons olive oil	2 sprigs of parsley
juice of 1 lemon	1 stalk celery, whole, or cut in half if
1 teaspoon sugar	it does not fit into saucepan
1 teaspoon salt	2 tablespoons chopped dill

Wash and slice the zucchini into diagonal slices ½-inch-thick. Put the slices in a lidded saucepan and add the water, oil, lemon juice, sugar, salt, peppercorns, coriander seeds, parsley and celery. Bring to the boil, lower the flame and mix well and simmer — covered — until barely tender, not more than 10 minutes. With a slotted spoon take out the zucchini and as few of the spices as possible to a shallow serving dish. Strain the liquid, discarding the celery, parsley and remaining spices. Add the dill to the sauce and pour over vegetables. Cool before serving.

Serves 6.

Baby Zucchini in Tomato Sauce
(Kalavasikas in Sos di Domates)

Zucchini and tomatoes is probably one of the most common vegetable combinations in the entire Mediterranean region, with the specific country of origin revealed only by the choice of seasonings. In Bulgaria we used parsley or dill.

2 pounds small zucchini	1 teaspoon salt
2 tablespoons light vegetable oil	½ teaspoon sugar
¼ cup light tomato puree	juice of half a lemon
¾ cup water	ground black pepper
1 celery stalk, whole or cut in half to fit the saucepan	2 tablespoons chopped parsley or dill

Wash and slice the zucchini diagonally about ½-inch-thick. In a saucepan large enough to hold all the ingredients, heat the oil, add the tomato puree, water, stalk of celery, salt, sugar and lemon juice. Cover and cook for 10 minutes. Add the sliced zucchini and cook until barely tender, not more than another 5 minutes. Uncover, remove the celery stalk and add a good grinding of pepper and the chopped parsley (or dill). Taste to rectify seasoning. Pour into serving dish and chill.

Serves 6.

Swiss Chard in Lemon Sauce
(Pazi in Salsa di Limon)

A thrifty vegetable that lends itself to two separate dishes at one go. The thin white stalks can be boiled with oil and lemon and a bit of sugar, as in this recipe, and eaten chilled. The broad, dark green leaves can be boiled and eaten like spinach or added to soup.

2 pounds Swiss chard	1 teaspoon salt
1 cup water	pinch of sugar
2 tablespoons olive oil	juice of 1 lemon

Wash the chard and slice the leafy part away from the thick white stems. (Reserve the leaves to cook like spinach in plenty of salted boiling water.) Cut the white stalks into ½-inch slices. Put them into a saucepan with the water, oil, salt, sugar and lemon juice, and cook for 7 or 8 minutes until barely cooked. Pour into a bowl and chill in the liquid before serving.

Serves 6.

Okra in Tomato Sauce
(Bamya Ilada con Domates)

Widely appreciated in the Balkans, this otherwise neglected vegetable is delicious cooked with tomatoes and eaten chilled. To retain its viscous juices, try to remove the crown without cutting into the pod. A good sharp knife should help.

2 pounds okra	1 tablespoon sugar
2 tablespoons vinegar	1 teaspoon salt
8 large tomatoes, peeled, seeded and chopped	juice of ½ lemon
3 tablespoons olive oil	2 tablespoons chopped fresh dill
½ cup water	freshly ground pepper

Wash and carefully trim the stems of the okra, without cutting into the vegetable. Cover them with hot water, add the vinegar and allow to stand for ¼ hour. Drain.

Peel the tomatoes by pouring boiling water over them and then slipping off skins. Remove seeds and chop the tomatoes coarsely. Heat the oil, add the tomatoes and ½ cup water, and cook gently for 15 minutes. Add the salt, sugar, lemon juice and the okra, cover and cook for ½ hour. Uncover, add the chopped dill and a grinding of pepper. Taste for seasoning and allow to cool in the liquid before serving.

Serves 6.

Leek with Olives
(Praza con Azeitunas)

Leeks are one of the most gentle members of the onion family, with a long history reaching way back to ancient times and today available only in cultivated form. Essential in soups, they lend themselves to a large variety of other uses as well. This delicious preparation is highlighted by salty black olives.

10 medium-sized leeks	1 teaspoon salt
2 tablespoons oil	pinch of sugar
1 tablespoon flour	15–20 black olives pitted and
3 to 4 tablespoons tomato paste	halved
mixed with ½ cup water	ground black pepper
2 tablespoons vinegar	

Wash, clean and chop off the tough green ends of the leeks. Cut the remaining white part into diagonal slices of a 2-inch width. Parboil for 3 minutes and drain.

Put the oil into a large heavy skillet and saute the drained leeks. Remove the leeks with a slotted spoon and set aside. Into the same pan, sprinkle the flour and cook for half a minute until it is golden. Carefully mix in the tomato paste-water mixture, the vinegar, salt and sugar and allow to cook over a low flame until slightly thickened.

Return the leeks to the pan, add the olives, cover and cook for another 10 minutes. Remove from the fire, pour the leeks with their sauce into a flat serving dish, add a good grinding of pepper and cool before serving.

Serves 6.

Artichokes Turkish Style
(Articho ala Turka)

The mellow taste of this dish is more than adequate compensation for the somewhat tedious work of trimming and cleaning the artichokes. The unusual combination of artichoke hearts and carrots is indigenous to the Balkans.

12 medium to large artichokes	2 carrots, sliced thinly
1 lemon, halved	1 slice lemon
a bowl of cold water to which has	½ teaspoon sugar
been added one tablespoon flour	1 teaspoon salt
and the juice of a lemon	1½ cups water
½ cup olive oil	

Cut away the tough leaves of the artichoke until you reach the heart. Cut away the choke of the heart with a sharp paring knife, leaving the bowl-shaped heart free of leaves and fuzzy choke. Rub the entire heart with lemon, and put the heart immediately into the bowl of cold water, in which has been dissolved the flour and the juice of an entire lemon. (This will prevent the artichoke from turning black.) Spread the olive oil in a wide, shallow pan large enough to hold the artichokes in one layer. Spread the carrots over the bottom, add the slice of lemon and sprinkle with sugar and salt. Add the artichokes hearts bottoms up, in one layer, and add the water. Cover the pan and bring to a boil over a medium fire.

Simmer for about ½ hour until the artichoke hearts are tender. Carefully remove the hearts with a slotted spoon and arrange bottoms up on a serving platter.

Boil the cooking liquid down to half its original quantity, and pour over artichokes. Chill before serving.

Serves 6.

Button Mushroom Stew
(Yachni di Champignones)

Small button mushrooms are one of the most delicate little vegetables you'll come across. Mild in themselves, they have a superb ability to pick up and lend taste to the foods they are cooked with. This recipe is somewhat unusual. Most often, mushrooms are sauteed with onions. Here they are stewed in their own juices with sweed red peppers and luscious black olives, then garnished with a touch of parsley. The result is a remarkably good blend of tastes. Serve at room temperature as an appetizer or warm over a bed of rice as a light meal.

1 large onion, coarsely chopped	5 ounces black olives (about 20),
3 tablespoons olive oil	pitted and halved
2 red peppers, seeded and cut into	1 teaspoon salt
½ -inch squares	freshly ground pepper
2 pounds small fresh mushrooms,	2 tablespoons chopped parsley
halved	

Use a large skillet with a cover. Fry the chopped onion uncovered in the olive oil until transparent. Add the peppers. Continue cooking for 5 minutes. Wash and halve the mushrooms with their stems and add to the pot. Mix well with peppers and onion, reduce the fire and cover and cook for another 10 minutes. Uncover. Add the pitted olives, salt, ground pepper and chopped parsley. Mix again, remove immediately from fire to a serving dish. Serve at room temperature.

Serves 6.

Brains with Boiled Mayonnaise
(Miyoyo con Agristada)

Calves' brains are the most delicate of the various types of brains on the market. Properly cooked, that is with all the membranes carefully removed, they positively melt in your mouth. Traditionally, we ate them as a festive first course, an alternative to the holiday fish. The mayonnaise-like sauce gives the mild morsels the necessary piquancy.

3 calves' brains	2 teaspoons flour
water to cover	2 additional cups water
4 tablespoons vinegar	juice of 1½ lemons
½ cup light vegetable oil	1 teaspoon salt
½ cup fresh water	½ teaspoon sugar
2 tablespoons chopped parsley	4 eggs, lightly beaten to a froth

Soak the brains in the water and vinegar for 1 hour. Clean the brains carefully, removing all film and membranes and cut each brain in half. Use a large saucepan with a cover. Heat the oil in the saucepan and saute the brains, uncovered, lightly. Add ½ cup fresh water, lower the flame, cover and cook for 10 minutes. Remove the cover. Add chopped parsley to the pan and cook for another 2 minutes. Remove the brains with slotted spoon to a deep serving dish and reserve the cooking liquid in the pan.

Put the flour into a deep bowl and slowly add the 2 cups of water, mixing continually to make sure it does not lump. Add the lemon juice, salt and sugar and the lightly beaten eggs. Spoon 3 tablespoons of the reserved cooking liquid into the bowl, mix well and add the entire mixture to the remaining cooking liquid in the saucepan. Cook over a low fire, mixing with a wooden spoon or whisk until the mixture begins to thicken slightly. It should have the consistency of thick cream. Remove from fire and pour over brains. Refrigerate and serve cold.

Serves 6.

Brains in Tomato Sauce
(Miyoyo con Domates)

Another version of brains — this time cubed, sauteed, cooked in a zesty tomato sauce, and, at the last minute, perked up with the always delightful combination of fresh dill, lemon juice and ground pepper.

3 calves' brains	pinch of sugar
water to cover	ground pepper
4 tablespoons vinegar	¼ cup water
4 tablespoons light vegetable oil	3 tablespoons chopped fresh dill
4 ripe tomatoes, peeled and thinly sliced	additional ground pepper
	juice of ½ lemon
1 teaspoon salt	

In a large bowl, cover the brains with water, add the vinegar and soak for 1 hour. Remove the film and membrane. Cut the brains into large cubes of about 1 inch. In a 2-inch-deep skillet (with cover) heat the oil and brown the brains lightly. Remove with a slotted spoon and set aside. Add the sliced tomatoes to the saucepan and cook until they are soft, for 3 or 4 minutes. Add salt, pinch of sugar and ground pepper. Replace the pieces of brain in the skillet atop the bed of tomatoes. Add the ¼ cup water, cover and simmer for 15 minutes. Uncover, add a generous sprinkling of chopped dill, ground pepper and lemon juice. Serve when cool.

Serves 6.

Brain Fritters
(Fritas di Miyoyo)

Soft on the inside, crisp and golden on the outside, these little brain *fritas* can be served with an *agristada* as a first course or with a potato or rice salad for a satisfying evening meal.

3 calves' brains	½ teaspoon nutmeg
water to cover	3 eggs
1 tablespoon vinegar	oil for deep frying
3 tablespoons flour	3 tablespoons chopped parsley
salt	5 lemon wedges
ground pepper	

Soak the brains in water and vinegar for 1 hour. Remove all film and membranes. In a saucepan cover the brains with fresh salted water, and parboil for 3 minutes. Drain. Cut the brains into small cubes of about ½ inch. In a large bowl, mix flour, salt, ground pepper, nutmeg and eggs. Add the pieces of brain and mix it all very well.

Pour enough oil to immerse the brain cube mixture into a heavy skillet and heat until sizzling hot. Drop in the mixture, tablespoon by tablespoon, and fry until golden. Drain on paper towels. If served as a first course add *agristada* (boiled mayonnaise, p. 98). Decorate with lemon wedges and a generous sprinkling of parsley.

Serves 6.

Yoghurt Soup
(Tarator)

A cool, tangy soup, most refreshing on a hot summer evening or as a midday snack. Fresh mint can be substituted for the dill for a rather different taste.

6 cups yoghurt	3 medium-sized cucumbers,
2 tablespoons vinegar	peeled and finely cubed
¼ cup olive oil	3 heaped tablespoons chopped
1 teaspoon salt	fresh dill
1 teaspoon sugar	½ cup chopped walnuts
3 garlic cloves, crushed	

Beat together the yoghurt, vinegar, oil, salt and sugar, either in an electric mixer or with a whisk. The mixture should be of the consistency of light cream. (If it seems too thick, add a little water.) Remove from the mixer, add the garlic, cubed cucumbers and chopped dill. Mix well and cool in the refrigerator.

Before serving, sprinkle with the chopped nuts.

Serves 6.

Calves' Trotter Soup
(Pacha)

For those who relish a robust, glutinous and flavorful soup, it is worth seeking out the butcher who sells calves' feet. Served with toasted garlic bread, this Sephardic standby makes an uncommonly good winter meal.

4 calves' feet	4–5 allspice kernels
6 cups water	½ teaspoon salt
1 onion, whole	6 garlic cloves, crushed
1 celery stalk, halved	5 grindings freshly ground pepper
1 carrot, halved	2 tablespoons chopped dill
3 sprigs of parsley	3 eggs
1 bay leaf	1 tablespoon white vinegar
10 peppercorns	

Have the butcher chop the calves' feet into 2½-inch slices. Wash them well and bring to the boil in a deep saucepan with the water, onion, celery, carrot, parsley, bay leaf, peppercorns, allspice kernels and salt. Simmer, covered, for 2 hours or more, until the meat falls away from the bones. Strain the liquid into a clean bowl. Discard bones and vegetables, picking out as best you can, however, the bone marrow and softer cartilage. Add these to the liquid and pour the entire mixture into a shallow pan and chill.

When chilled, remove the layer of fat that has formed on the top. Return contents of pan to a saucepan, add the crushed garlic cloves, heat to boiling point and add ground pepper and chopped dill. Taste, correct seasoning.

Separately, in a small bowl beat the eggs lightly, add the vinegar and a ladleful or two of the soup. Mix well and return to the saucepan. Cook over a very low flame until it starts to thicken (do not allow to boil) and serve immediately.

Serves 6.·

Eggs Sauteed with Tomatoes, Peppers and White Cheese
(Guevos con Domates, Pipiritzas i Ceso Blanco)

An infinite number of egg dishes using peppers and tomatoes must have come out of Spain. In this Bulgarian version the eggs are mixed with feta cheese before being poured over the sauteed vegetables.

3 tablespoons light vegetable oil
2 green peppers, seeded and sliced in rounds
2 red peppers, seeded and sliced in rounds
4 tomatoes, peeled, seeded and sliced
8 eggs
1 cup feta cheese, crumbled
½ teaspoon ground pepper
salt (optional)

Prepare all the ingredients. Warm the oil in a heavy skillet and saute the red and green peppers gently. Add the tomatoes and stir. Cook for a few minutes until the tomatoes begin to water and lower the heat.

In a mixing bowl, lightly beat the eggs, add the crumbled cheese and fold together. Pour the eggs over the tomato-pepper mixture in the skillet. Add the pepper (and salt, if necessary) and cook until the eggs begin to set, occasionally stirring with a wooden spoon. Serve straight from the hot skillet.

Serves 6.

Jellied Whiting
(Jelatina di Peshcado)

This fish dish almost always began our Sabbath evening meal. Simmered whole, colorfully garnished with carrots and celery stalks and leaves, and set in aspic, its aristocratic elegance eminently suits the dignity of the occasion.

1 fresh whiting (or other firm-fleshed fish) weighing 2 to 2½ pounds	1 celery stalk, with leaves
	1 whole onion, peeled
	10 peppercorns
2 cups water	1 teaspoon salt
2 tablespoons light vegetable oil	juice of ½ lemon
2 tablespoons vinegar	pinch of sugar
2 carrots, sliced	

Have the fish cleaned, but retain the head. In a large fish kettle or stewing pot (large enough to hold the fish whole), boil together the water, oil, vinegar, sliced carrots, celery, onion, peppercorns and salt, for 20 minutes.

Add the fish to the kettle and simmer gently for about 20–25 minutes. Remove the pot from the fire and allow the fish to cool in its cooking liquid. When it is cool enough to handle, gently lift the fish from the cooking liquid, keeping it whole, and place it on its serving dish. The dish should be deep enough to allow for the stock to be poured over the fish without spilling. Remove the skin from the fish, and garnish with slices of the cooked carrot and celery leaves.

Strain the stock, and cook again for another five minutes. Add the lemon juice, sugar and taste for seasoning. Pour the stock over the fish, and chill for a few hours before serving. The stock will have jellied by serving time.

Serves 4–6.

Fish with Boiled Mayonnaise
(Peshcado con Agristada)

Depending on whether you use a whole fish or steaks, the appearance changes, but never the taste. This is a slightly peppery taste which is given its distinctive Sephardic touch by the traditional *agristada*.

1 whiting (or any other firm white-fleshed fish) weighing 2½ pounds with head	1 teaspoon salt
	3 eggs, lightly beaten
	pinch of salt
3 cups water	white ground pepper
1 carrot, whole	juice of 1½ lemons
1 celery stalk and leaves, whole	½ teaspoon sugar
3 sprigs of parsley	1 tablespoon oil
2 tablespoons vegetable oil	3 tablespoons chopped parsley
10 peppercorns	

Clean the fish without removing the head.

In a fish kettle or stewing pot large enough to hold the whole fish boil the water, carrot, celery stalk, parsley sprigs, oil, peppercorns and salt for 15 or 20 minutes.

Add the entire fish to the kettle, lower the heat, and simmer gently for another 20–25 minutes. When cool enough to handle, remove the fish and arrange on a serving platter. Peel off the upper layer of skin and discard. Strain the cooking liquid and return to heat. Boil the liquid down to half the original amount. While the cooking liquid is reducing, lightly beat the eggs in a separate bowl, add to them a pinch of salt, a grinding of white pepper, the lemon juice and sugar. When the liquid in which the fish has been cooked is reduced to half, stir 2 tablespoons of it into the beaten egg mixture. Lower the heat, and pour the egg mixture into the fish broth, stirring continuously until the broth thickens. Do not allow to boil.

As soon as it thickens, remove immediately from the heat and pour over the fish. Allow to chill before serving. Just before serving, heat 1 tablespoon oil in a small skillet and add some finely chopped parsley. Cook for 1 minute, and spoon the mixture in a pattern over the chilled fish.

Serves 4–6.

Baked Red Snapper
(Peshcado al Orno)

There is a marvelous group of fish dishes prepared with a lively supporting cast of vegetables and spices: onions, tomatoes, celery, peppers, parsley and dill. Individually or in combination, they bolster the flavor of every fish. The lovely red snapper in this recipe makes one of the most elegant variations, but a simpler fish, such as sea bream or even the humble mackerel will do very nicely.

1 red snapper, weighing 2–3 pounds	4 large tomatoes, sliced into ⅛ inch slices
½ lemon	1 teaspoon salt
salt	½ teaspoon pepper
2 celery stalks, whole with leaves	3–4 tablespoons chopped parsley
¼ cup oil	6 lemon wedges
2 onions, sliced finely	

Have the fish cleaned without removing its head. Rub it all over with lemon and salt. Put the celery with its leaves inside the fish.

Spread the bottom of a baking dish with 1½ tablespoons of the oil, add about ¾ of the sliced onion and ¾ of the sliced tomatoes, salt and pepper. Sprinkle with half the parsley. Make two sharp, not too deep, diagonal incisions on the uppermost side of fish and lay it over the vegetables. Pour the remaining oil over the fish, arrange the lemon wedges on top, surround them with the remaining sliced tomatoes and onions. Sprinkle with the remaining parsley, cover with foil and bake for 20 minutes in a 375° oven. Remove the foil, return the fish to the oven and cook for another 20–25 minutes. Serve warm or cooled.

Serves 4–6.

Stewed Fish
(Peshcado Plaki 1)

Another variation on the classic fish and vegetable theme. This version, in which tomato paste and a pinch of sugar are added to the sauce, is briefly stewed and makes an ideal choice for the cook in a hurry.

6 slices halibut (or other not too bony, firm white fish), in 1½-inch slices
¼ cup olive oil
2 onions, sliced thinly
4 ripe tomatoes, chopped
2 tablespoons tomato paste
2 stalks celery, chopped

1 teaspoon salt
½ teaspoon sugar
1 bay leaf
1 cup water
juice of 1 lemon
2 tablespoons chopped dill
5 grindings fresh pepper

In a deep skillet, large enough to hold the fish and all the vegetables, heat the oil and saute the onions slightly. Add the chopped tomatoes, the tomato paste, celery, salt, sugar and bay leaf. Add the water and cook for 10 minutes over high heat. Add the slices of fish; lower the heat and poach until cooked, 10–12 minutes. Take the pan from the heat and add the lemon juice. Arrange the slices of fish on a serving dish, the tomato mixture remaining in the skillet. Add the chopped dill and pepper to the sauce. Taste, correct the seasoning, and pour over the fish. Let it stand a few hours before serving at room temperature.

Serves 6.

Hake in Tomato and Wine Sauce (Peshcado Plaki 2)

This dish can be made with hake, mackerel, halibut or other firm-fleshed fish. It is a good idea to refrigerate the fish for at least half a day to allow it to absorb the subtle flavor of the tomato and wine sauce. Then remove it an hour or so before serving at room temperature.

1 hake, or other firm-fleshed fish, weighing about 3 pounds, sliced	1 dill-pickled cucumber, sliced thinly
3 tablespoons flour	6 ripe tomatoes, pureed
4 tablespoons light vegetable oil	1 teaspoon salt
1 onion, sliced thinly	½ teaspoon sugar
1 carrot, sliced thinly	½ teaspoon pepper
½ small celeriac (celery root) peeled and sliced thinly	2 bay leaves
	½ cup red wine

Clean and slice the fish into slices about 1 inch thick. Wash, towel dry, lightly dust with flour and fry on both sides in hot oil until cooked. Drain the slices on paper towels and arrange in a shallow serving casserole.

Blanch the sliced onion, carrot, celeriac and pickle in a boiling salted water for 5 minutes. Drain in a colander. Puree the tomatoes in a blender and pour into a saucepan. Add the drained vegetables, salt, sugar, pepper, bay leaves and red wine. Cook over high heat until it boils. Lower the heat and cook for 5–7 minutes. Taste and correct seasoning. Pour the sauce over the fish and cool 12 hours or more in the refrigerator before serving.

Serves 6.

Cold Bass with Mayonnaise Sauce (Peshcado Ilado con Mayonaisa)

Beautifully embellished with yellow lemon wedges and pitted black olives, this whole bass dish is a striking opener for the most gala of meals. To this day I take special pleasure in serving it.

The Fish:

1 fresh bass weighing between 2 and 3 pounds
2 cups water
2 tablespoons white wine vinegar
1 onion, whole
2 carrots, scraped and sliced in 1½-inch slices
2 celery stalks with leaves, scraped and sliced in 1½-inch slices
2 sprigs parsley
10 peppercorns
1 teaspoon salt

mayonnaise (see recipe below)
lemon wedges
black olives (pitted)

Mayonnaise:

2 whole eggs plus one yolk
1 teaspoon Dijon mustard
1 teaspoon salt
pinch of sugar
1 cup olive oil
juice of ½ lemon
full bunch finely chopped parsley leaves

Clean the fish without removing the head. In a fish kettle or pot large enough to hold the entire fish bring to a boil the water, vinegar, onion, carrots, celery, parsley, peppercorns and salt. Cook for 10 minutes. Lower the fish carefully into the pan. Add water to cover, if necessary. Reduce the heat and poach the fish over a low heat for 20–25 minutes. Allow to cool in the cooking liquid.

Carefully remove the fish from the bouillon and place on a serving platter. Gently remove the upper skin, but leave on the head. Spread the mayonnaise over the fish and garnish with lemon wedges and whole, pitted olives.

Mayonnaise
In a blender or food processor (using the plastic blade) place the whole eggs and the egg yolk, add the mustard, salt and sugar, and begin to blend. Add the oil in a very slow stream. Halfway through, add the lemon juice and slowly pour in the remaining oil. Remove the mayonnaise to a bowl and work in the finely chopped parsley. Spread over fish.

Serves 6.

Cold Bass in Lemon and Dill Sauce (Peshcado Ilado in Sos di Limon i Dill)

Fresh sea bass, gray mullet and halibut are all excellent choices for this gratifying dish. The boiled fish is flavored by an enticing, sultry sauce made by reducing the cooking liquid to its essence and adding lemon juice and olive oil, crushed garlic, salt, sugar and the ever-flavorful dill.

1 fresh bass (about 3 pounds)	**The Sauce:**
3 cups water	juice of 1 lemon
2 tablespoons white wine vinegar	3 tablespoons olive oil
2 celery stalks, with leaves, chopped coarsely	2 garlic cloves, crushed
1 yellow onion, peeled	1 teaspoon salt
½ teaspoon salt	½ teaspoon sugar
	3 tablespoons fresh chopped dill

Clean and cut the fish into 1½-inch slices. Reserve the head. In a fish kettle, or ordinary saucepan large enough to hold the fish slices, bring to a boil 3 cups water, the vinegar, celery stalks, onion, fish head and salt. Cook together for 10 minutes. Remove the fish head and gently lower the pieces of fish into the pan. Cook over low heat for 10–12 minutes. Lift the pieces of fish from the pan with a slotted spoon and arrange them on a deep serving dish. Strain the cooking liquid and replace it in the saucepan. Cook over high heat until the liquid is reduced to ½ cup. For the sauce combine the lemon juice with the oil, crushed garlic cloves, salt, sugar and chopped dill. Add the reduced cooking liquid and pour over the fish. Allow to cool before serving.

Serves 6.

Stewed Striped Bass
(Gewetch di Peshcado)

This dish can be prepared with striped bass, turbot or hake. One of my favorites, it is a veritable summer symphony, featuring a full array of vegetables and spices and well worth the chopping and slicing, boiling and sauteeing required before it is all snugly arranged in a baking dish and placed in the oven. The end result is a marvel to behold and a wonder to taste.

3–4 pounds fresh striped bass
2 large potatoes
4 tablespoons olive oil
2 yellow onions, peeled and sliced into thin rings
2 celery stalks, chopped coarsely
2 carrots, scraped and thinly sliced
2 green peppers, seeded and chopped into thin rings
2 pounds tomatoes, peeled, seeded and sliced
2 ounces uncooked green peas, shelled or frozen

2 ounces fresh green beans, sliced diagonally
1½ teaspoons salt
1 teaspoon pepper
2 bay leaves
5 kernels allspice
½ teaspoon sugar
2 tablespoons olive oil
salt
1 lemon, sliced thinly
4 tablespoons chopped parsley

Clean and slice the fish into 2½-inch-wide slices. Reserve the head.

Parboil the potatoes for 5–7 minutes, peel and slice thinly.

In a large, heavy skillet, heat the olive oil and saute the sliced onions, chopped celery, sliced carrots and pepper rings for 5 minutes. Remove with a slotted spoon to a large mixing bowl.

Into the same skillet, add the tomatoes, cook for a minute or two, then add the peas and the string beans. Continue cooking for another 3–5 minutes and remove with a slotted spoon to the bowl with the other vegetables. To the vegetables in the mixing bowl, add salt, the ground pepper, bay leaves, allspice kernels, sugar and 2 tablespoons of the parsley. Combine it all well.

Spread this vegetable mix on the bottom of a deep baking dish, large enough to hold the vegetables and fish. Insert the potato slices among the vegetables and arrange the pieces of fish on top, including the head. Drip another tablespoon or two of olive oil over the fish. Sprinkle salt over the fish, place the lemon slices on top and sprinkle the remaining chopped parsley over it all. Cover with aluminum foil and bake in a 375° oven for 20 minutes. Uncover, and bake for another 15 minutes. Serve warm or cold.

Serves 8.

EGG AND CHEESE DISHES

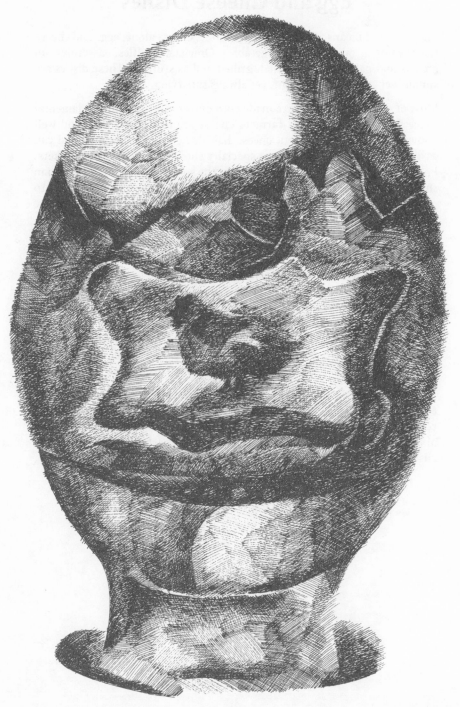

Jean david

Egg and Cheese Dishes

The ways and means are infinite. Eggs alone, cheese alone, eggs and cheese together or in tandem with vegetables. Omelets, souffles, casseroles, *au gratins* and patties. Baked, fried, grilled and as stuffing. These dishes are simple, yet sophisticated, light, yet always satisfying.

Most of our cheese dishes are made with one or more of four fundamental cheeses. Cream cheese and farmers cheese are readily available and well known. The salty Greek feta cheese has also come into its own and can easily be obtained in Mideastern specialty shops and many supermarkets. For this reason, I have substituted it for the somewhat creamier Bulgarian sheep's cheese we used at home — kept in a crock with brine or milk to preserve its moisture and delay fermentation — as they are really quite close in taste.

Katchkeval is a salty yellow cheese with a somewhat sharp flavor and a tendency to crumble. Though a staple in the Balkans and the Middle East, it may be difficult to come by elsewhere, so you'll have to find substitutes. I haven't suggested any single alternative in the recipes because there is no cheese that I know of that is really similar. Parmesan perhaps comes closest in its sharpness and consistency, while cheddar or cheshire may make interesting variations. But on the whole I think personal taste will have to guide you. Only, whatever you select, make sure that it's strong enough in its own right to give the otherwise mild dishes the necessary zing.

In Bulgaria, these egg and cheese dishes tended to be served up on summer evenings, and I still associate them with long summer holidays in the country. Today, I most often serve them for lunch when I have guests, and of course on *Shavuot* (the Feast of Weeks), when dairy foods are customary.

Baked Eggs
(Guevos in Haminados)

A staple in our home, baked eggs were regularly eaten for Saturday morning breakfast. They were baked for the whole night in a slow Sabbath oven, but three or four hours of cooking works just as well. They are the creamiest of creamy, with only the tiniest hint of onion peel in the taste, and the egg whites turned a smooth caramel brown. Try to remember to save your onion peels. When you have collected enough of them, bake a large batch of eggs. They keep forever, though they'll be gone sooner.

1 large porcelanized casserole to hold as many eggs as to fill comfortably
eggs, whole and uncracked
brown onion peel, to line the casserole and cover the layer of eggs

1 tablespoon salt for every 15 eggs
1 tablespoon coffee for every 15 eggs
2 tablespoons oil for every 15 eggs
water to cover

Line a casserole with onion peel, place whole unbroken eggs (as many as you want) in the casserole; cover with another layer of onion peel. Sprinkle in salt, coffee and oil, pour enough water to cover the eggs. Cover and cook on a low heat or in a slow oven for 3–4 hours. The water will have evaporated, leaving the eggs a deep brown color.

When peeled, the eggs should be light brown inside, and have a smooth buttery texture.

Serve with a sprinkling of salt and a grinding of pepper.

Eggs Sauteed with Onions
(Guevos con Sivoya)

This is realy an easy to prepare, one-pan Sephardic omelet in which the eggs are lightly scrambled over sauteed onions. The sweeter the onions, the sweeter the dish.

12 eggs	2 tablespoons oil or margarine, for
4 tablespoons milk	frying
1½ teaspoons salt	2 large onions, sliced into thin rings
½ teaspoon ground pepper	additional ground pepper

In a mixing bowl beat eggs, milk, salt and pepper. Set aside.

Heat the oil or margarine in a heavy skillet and saute the onions lightly. Add the eggs, mix the onions with a wooden spoon and allow to cook until the mixture sets. Serve immediately with a sprinkling of ground pepper.

Serves 6.

Eggs and Katchkeval Cheese
(Guevos con Kashkaval)

Katchkeval was never bought by the ounce but by the wheel, seven or eight pounds at a time. So the slices were generous, though you can cut thinner for a less cheesy dish. In this recipe, slices of cheese are lightly fried in oil or margarine, then individually topped with an egg that is allowed to set sunny side up.

6 teaspoons margarine or oil	6 eggs
6 slices katchkeval, or other hard	salt
yellow cheese, each ½ inch thick	paprika

This egg dish can be prepared either in individual flameproof dishes or all together in a skillet.

Melt the oil or margarine, either 1 teaspoon each in individual dish or all together in a heavy skillet. Add the sliced cheese to each dish and cook for a minute or two. Break an egg on top of each piece of cheese and cook until the egg is set. Add a pinch of salt and paprika, and serve immediately before the cheese hardens.

Serves 6.

Eggs Melted with White Cheese (Guevos con Ceso Blanco)

The mild farmers cheese and salty feta combine to just the right savoriness in our Sephardic version of the cheese omelet.

6 eggs	2 tablespoons margarine or oil
3 tablespoons milk	salt (optional)
½ cup farmers cheese, crumbled	ground pepper
½ cup feta cheese, crumbled	

Beat the eggs lightly and mix in the milk. In another bowl crumble both the farmers cheese and the feta cheese. Pour the eggs over and fold together well.

In a frying pan heat the oil or margarine. Pour in the egg-cheese mixture, and allow to cook over a fairly low heat, stirring with a spatula or a wooden spoon.

When the eggs are set, remove from the fire, taste, add some salt if necessary and a sprinkling of ground black pepper. Serve quickly, straight from the frying pan.

Serves 6.

Souffle of White Cheese
(Souffle di Ceso Blanco)

Custardy and slightly pungent, this farmers cheese and sour cream souffle has a wonderful flavor — something like a sugarless cheese cake. Served with a mild tomato sauce, it makes a light and pleasant lunchtime meal.

1 cup milk	5 eggs, whole
2 tablespoons butter or margarine	salt
pinch of salt	nutmeg
2 tablespoons flour	½ cup grated katchkeval
2 cups farmers cheese, crumbled	buttered souffle dish
½ cup sour cream	

In a saucepan warm the milk, add the butter or margarine to melt and a pinch of salt. Put the flour into a small bowl and add 2 or 3 tablespoons of the warm milk to dilute the flour. Add the mixture to the saucepan, whisking it with a wire whisk constantly until the mixture starts to thicken.

Remove the mixture from the heat, add the cheese, sour cream and the unbeaten eggs one by one. Add salt to taste and a good grating of nutmeg.

Butter a souffle dish, gently pour in the mixture and sprinkle the grated katchkeval over the top.

Place in shallow pan of hot water, and bake in a 350° oven for 1–1½ hours. Serve immediately.

Serves 6.

Grilled White Cheese
(Ceso Blanco Asado)

Our white cheese came from the same family as the Greek feta, and grilled it was a treat for us. Feta is available today in most supermarkets, and certainly in Greek and Mideastern specialty shops.

6 slices feta cheese, each slice about ½ inch thick	aluminum foil
oil for greasing	6 slices toast
	ground pepper

Oil 6 sheets of aluminum foil, each large enough to wrap a slice of cheese into a neat parcel. Grill or broil the wrapped slices for about 5 minutes, turning once.

Turn each parcel out onto a slice of hot toast and grind some fresh pepper on top before serving.

Serves 6.

Breaded Katchkeval
(Kashkaval Pane)

When fried quickly, the cheese retains a firm, chewy consistency. This recipe calls for slicing the cheese, but if you cube it, the little tidbits make a novel accompaniment to cocktails.

6 slices katchkeval or other hard, yellow cheese, in ½-inch-thick slices flour	2 eggs, beaten with 1 tablespoon water bread crumbs oil

Dust each slice of cheese with flour. Dip each into the eggs which have been beaten with water. Coat each slice with the bread crumbs. Fry in hot oil on both sides and drain on a paper napkin.

Serve immediately with green salad.

Serves 6.

Batter-Fried Katchkeval
(Kashkaval Pane)

These golden batter-fried fritters make a heartier dish than the previous one. Served with a vegetable or potato salad, they are filling enough for a light meal.

6 slices katchkeval or other hard, yellow cheese, each ½ inch thick	½ cup milk
3 tablespoons flour	1 tablespoon butter
1 egg	2 tablespoons light vegetable oil

Put the flour into a wide bowl and add the egg. With a wire whisk, mix the two together. Add the milk slowly and mix until the batter is smooth. Allow to stand for about 1 hour.

Heat the butter and oil in a large frying pan. Dip each cheese slice into the batter, and fry on both sides until light brown. Remove to drain on absorbent paper and serve immediately.

Serves 6.

Grilled Katchkeval
(Kashkaval Asado)

In our version of "grilled cheese," the cheese is grilled and the bread toasted separately. When they are put together, the toast is crisp on both sides and the cheese hot and melting — so you bite into a marvelous contrast of textures.

6 slices katchkeval or other hard yellow cheese, in ½-inch-thick slices

oil for greasing aluminum foil
6 slices toast
1 teaspoon paprika (sweet)

Oil 6 sheets of aluminum foil each large enough to wrap a slice of cheese into a neat parcel. Grill or broil for about 5–7 minutes, turning it once. Unwrap and turn out onto a slice of hot toast, sprinkle with sweet paprika and serve immediately.

Serves 6.

Casserole of Green Peppers and Feta Cheese
(Pipiritzas con Ceso)

This rich casserole is made by alternating layers of grilled green peppers, crumbled feta cheese, and a katchkeval sauce. Served with plenty of fresh bread, it is a wonderful summer meal.

12–14 firm, unblemished green peppers	salt
1½ cups milk	ground pepper
4 tablespoons margarine or butter	1 cup katchkeval cheese, grated
3 tablespoons flour	3 eggs, whole
	1 cup feta cheese, crumbled

Grill the peppers over an open flame if available, or under the broiler until they are black on all sides. (Turn as each side becomes black.) Rub off the black peel, washing under running water. Remove the crown, cut each pepper into quarters and scrape out the seeds and fibers within. Set aside.

In a small pan warm the milk. Melt 3 tablespoons of the margarine or butter in a larger saucepan, add the flour, mix and then slowly add the warmed milk, whisking with a wire whisk until the mixture thickens. Remove from fire and add salt and ground pepper, the katchkeval cheese and eggs, beating in one by one.

Butter with margarine or butter a large shallow baking dish. Arrange ⅓ of the peppers in a layer, sprinkle ⅓ of the crumbled feta cheese over them and pour ⅓ of the cheese bechamel over the entire layer. Repeat with a second, then a third layer of peppers, cheese and bechamel. Finish with the bechamel. Dot with the remaining tablespoon of butter. Bake in a 350° oven for ¾ hour.

Serves 8.

Cheese-Stuffed Green Peppers
(Pipiritzas con Ceso)

This dish amply repays the cook who takes the trouble to become adept. The green peppers are grilled and peeled, filled with a creamy mixture of farmers, feta and katchkeval cheese, rolled in flour and fried to a nice brown. Crisp on the outside, creamy within, they make a wonderful first course.

12–14 green peppers	2 eggs, lightly beaten
1¼ cups feta cheese, crumbled	2–3 tablespoons flour
1¼ cups farmers cheese, crumbled	2 tablespoons margarine
¾ cups katchkeval cheese, grated	2 tablespoons oil

Grill the peppers over an open flame if you have one or under the broiler until black. Rub off the blackened skin, leaving the crowns intact. Make an incision along the side of the pepper, and gently remove the seeds. Take special care to leave the peppers otherwise intact.

In a large bowl mix the three cheeses together with two forks. Mix in the beaten eggs and gently stuff each pepper with the mixture.

Roll each pepper in flour. Two or three tablespoons of flour should be enough, but if you need more, add.

In a deep, heavy skillet melt the margarine with the oil. Fry as many peppers as can fit and be turned in the skillet at one time, turning each carefully until they are well browned and crisp on all sides. Remove to heated serving dish and repeat until all the peppers are well cooked. Serve immediately.

Serves 8.

Baked Eggplant and Peppers with Cheese Sauce
(Pipiritzas in Mirindgenas con Ceso)

Strips of smokey eggplant alternating with grilled green peppers are bound together in a creamy cheese sauce. Be sure to use a dish large enough to hold the vegetables in one layer.

2 large eggplants
12 green peppers
3 tablespoons butter or margarine
1¼ cups feta cheese, crumbled

1¼ cups farmers cheese, crumbled
¾ cups katchkeval cheese, grated
4 eggs

Grill the eggplants and peppers over an open flame, if available, or under the broiler until each is black on all sides. The eggplant should be soft inside. Peel the eggplant while still warm and set in a colander to drain for ½ hour. When drained, slice into long thin strips.

Rub the blackened skins off the peppers, remove the crowns, slice each in half and remove the inner seeds and pith.

In a heavy skillet, melt 2 tablespoons of the butter or margarine, and saute the peppers. Remove with a slotted spoon to separate dish. Add the eggplant strips to the skillet and saute for a few minutes. Remove from heat and set aside.

In a large mixing bowl blend together the cheeses. Add the eggs and mix well. In a buttered baking dish, arrange the eggplant and peppers along the bottom, pour the cheese-egg mixture over and dot with the remaining tablespoon of butter. Bake for 40–45 minutes in a 375° oven until golden.

Serves 8.

Baked Chopped Eggplant
(Baked with Cheese)
(Almudroti)

This is actually an *au gratin* of eggplant and cheese, and like all *au gratin*s is not only a graceful way of presenting vegetables, but a very tasty one. Surprising as it may seem, the cheese actually strengthens and reinforces the taste of the eggplant.

1 large or 2 medium-sized eggplants	¼ teaspoon sugar
1½ cups cream cheese	¾ cup katchkeval, grated
4 eggs	2 tablespoons margarine or light vegetable oil
½ teaspoon salt	

Grill the eggplant over an open flame, if you have one, or under the broiler until it is soft and black. While still warm, peel and stand in a colander to drain for ½ hour. Chop finely.

In a mixer blend the chopped eggplant with the cream cheese. Beat in the eggs, one by one, and add salt, sugar and half the katchkeval.

Spread the mixture on a buttered baking dish, dot with margarine or oil and bake in a 350° oven. After about 20 minutes, remove and sprinkle the rest of the katchkeval on top and finish baking until golden, about 20 more minutes. Serve warm, accompanied by a salad. This dish can serve as light meal in itself.

Serves 6.

Baked Zucchini with Cheese
(Kalavasikas al Orno)

Parboiling vegetables in milk tenderizes them — even rejuvenating some that already seem to wilt. This baked zucchini and cheese is an exceptionally delicate dish. I like to serve it for a light summer lunch; for an eye-appealing and tangy complement I add a fresh red tomato salad.

3 pounds small zucchini	¼ teaspoon sugar
¾ cup milk	¼ teaspoon nutmeg
1 cup cream cheese	½ teaspoon pepper
1¼ cups katchkeval cheese, grated	4 eggs
1 teaspoon salt	2 tablespoons butter or margarine

Wash, scrape and cube the zucchini. Parboil for 5 minutes in the milk and drain.

In a mixing bowl blend the cream cheese with half of the grated katchkeval, the salt, sugar, grating of nutmeg and pepper. Beat in the eggs one by one. Add the drained marrows and mix well.

Preheat the oven to 350°.

In a buttered baking dish spread the mixture and dot the surface with butter or margarine. Place in oven to bake. After about 20 minutes remove from oven, sprinkle the top with the remaining grated katchkeval and finish cooking until golden and crisp, another 20–25 minutes.

Serves 8.

Baked Zucchini with Cheese and Tomatoes
(Kalavasikas con Domates al Orno)

The zucchini are sliced thin, lightly floured, and fried until golden. They they are placed in alternating layers with tomatoes — each bringing out the taste of the other — and the whole is bound together by the cheese. Serve with a green salad.

6–8 medium-sized zucchini	1 tablespoon tomato puree
2–3 tablespoons flour	½ cup water
3 tablespoons light vegetable oil	salt
4 ripe tomatoes	pinch of sugar
1½ cups feta cheese, crumbled	½ cup katchkeval cheese, grated

Preheat oven to 350°.

Wash, scrape and thinly slice the zucchini lengthwise. Heat the oil in a skillet, dust each slice of zucchini with flour and fry in oil until golden. Drain on paper towels.

Wash, and slice the tomatoes. Crumble the feta cheese.

In a greased baking dish arrange one layer of zucchini, top it with a layer of sliced tomatoes and sprinkle over ½ cup of the crumbled feta cheese. Repeat the procedure twice more and top with a layer of zucchini.

Dilute the tomato puree with the water, add salt and sugar and pour over the zucchini. Sprinkle grated katchkeval across the top. Bake in a heated oven of 350° for 40 minutes.

Serves 6.

Zucchini Stuffed with White Cheese (Kalavasikas Ienas con Ceso)

Here are brought together the best of the garden and the best of the dairy. Stuffed with a mixture of farmers cheese and dill, and baked in a creamy bechamel sauce, these zucchini are positively luscious.

8–10 medium-sized zucchini
1 cup farmers cheese, crumbled
2 eggs
1 teapoon salt
2 tablespoons fresh chopped dill

2 tablespoons butter or margarine
1 tablespoon flour
½ cup milk
freshly ground black pepper

Preheat the oven to 350°.

Wash and scrape the zucchini. Chop off both ends, slice lengthwise and remove the seeds. With a carrot peeler, hollow a groove the length of each half. Sprinkle with salt and pour over hot water to cover. Allow to stand for ½ hour. Drain.

While the zucchini are draining mix the cheese, eggs, salt and dill in a small bowl.

Fill the drained zucchini with the cheese mixture.

Melt 1 tablespoon of the butter or margarine in a small saucepan, mix in the flour and add milk. Cook over low heat. When the bechamel thickens, remove from heat. Arrange the stuffed zucchini in a single layer on a shallow greased baking dish and carefully spoon a bit of bechamel over each.

Dot with the remaining tablespoon of butter or margarine, sprinkle black pepper over the top and bake for about 35–40 minutes until it forms a light crust.

Serves 8.

Baked Spinach with Cheese
(Spinaka con Ceso al Orno)

The melting cheese streaks through the spinach like the lighter colors through a dark Italian marble. The important thing is to dry the spinach to the very last drop; otherwise it will be soggy. If you must use frozen spinach, sqeeze out all the water with your hands, but you should realize that you'll lose the marbling, which is a pity. Serve with yoghurt, as I do.

2 pounds fresh spinach	¾ cup katchkeval cheese, grated
3 eggs	¼ teaspoon nutmeg
1 cup feta cheese, crumbled	½ cup butter or margarine
1 cup farmers cheese, crumbled	yoghurt (optional)

Wash and drain the spinach well. Chop finely and allow to dry for as long as possible.

In a mixing bowl, lightly beat the eggs, add the crumbled feta cheese, the crumbled farmers cheese, half of the grated katchkeval cheese and a grinding of nutmeg. Add the spinach and mix well.

Spread the mixture into a buttered baking dish, dot with butter or margarine and bake in a 370° oven for 20 minutes. Remove from oven, and sprinkle the rest of the katchkeval across the top. Continue baking until golden brown, another 20–25 minutes. Serve with yoghurt on the side.

Serves 6.

Potatoes Stuffed with White Cheese (Kartophis in Chidos con Ceso)

A wonderfully hearty dish that we as children always adored. Large Idaho potatoes will make it even better.

8 large potatoes, whole, washed, unpeeled
1 cup milk
1 slice stale bread, crust removed
2 cups farmers cheese, crumbled
¾ cup feta cheese, crumbled

¾ cups katchkeval cheese, grated
2 eggs
2 tablespoons chopped dill
salt and pepper
sour cream for garnish

Boil the potatoes whole and unpeeled until about half done. Peel, slice in half, and carefully scoop out a deep tablespoon of the potato, reserving the scooped out portion. Soak the bread in milk, squeeze dry and crumble, reserving the milk.

In a mixing bowl, mix the cheeses (using only ½ the katchkeval), eggs, crumbled bread, chopped dill, the scooped out part of the potatoes, salt and pepper. Stuff the potatoes with the mixture, piling loosely into a mound atop the potato. Arrange the potatoes in a buttered baking dish and sprinkle the remaining katchkeval over the tops. Pour the milk around the potatoes and bake in a 375° oven until the potatoes are soft, and the milk is absorbed. Serve with sour cream.

Serves 8.

Potato Rissoles with Cheese
(Fritas de Kartof con Ceso)

Made with cheese, these sliced and fried potato rolls are an extension of the simpler potato patty. They go very well with a simple poached or fried egg.

1 pound potatoes, whole, washed, unpeeled	½ cup katchkeval cheese, grated
	salt and pepper
2 eggs, beaten	2 tablespoons flour
2 tablespoons butter	frying oil

Boil the potatoes whole and unpeeled until well cooked. Peel and puree the potatoes in a mixer making sure there are no lumps. Beat in the eggs, butter, cheese, salt and pepper.

Form the mixture into a long roll of about 2-inches diameter. Cut the roll into slices one-inch thick.

Dust each slice with flour and fry in hot oil until golden. Remove with a slotted spoon and arrange on absorbent paper to drain. Serve hot.

About 18–20 rissoles.

MEAT

Meat

Veal, beef and lamb — these are the meats that most frequented our table. The veal and beef were always of the highest quality, butcher-bought, and from calves and cows that had been free fed on open green pastures. The lamb was always young, succulent and tender when it appeared in the early spring. And we avoided the tougher mutton.

Our meat, like our poultry, was prepared in quite a number of ways, sometimes ground and made into meatballs and patties, sometimes cubed and cooked with vegetables, and sometimes cooked in large chunks, though these were more often pot roasted than oven roasted.

Most of the dishes in this section are actually stews, goulashes or casseroles of sorts. Meat and rice combinations are characteristic of the Balkans — as a way of flavoring the rice as well as the meat — and there are recipes here for a shoulder or rack of lamb with rice and for a highly unusual but delicious pilaf of innards.

The most pervasive and versatile vegetables used, finding their way with almost every type of meat, are peppers and tomatoes. But beef is also cooked with cabbage and an abundance of onions as well as with the robust eggplant. Veal, always perked up with lemon, is generally made with the more delicate vegetables, of which the veal with artichoke hearts is representative. Lamb with spinach is another apt combination. Tongue also appeared on our table quite frequently, and I have given recipes for tongue with garlic and tongue with olives. Garlic, by the way, sometimes functioned not simply as seasoning, but practically as a vegetable in itself, as in the lamb with fresh onions and garlic, where it is used in very large amounts.

Most of the dishes here are updated. That is, in the recipes I inherited, vegetables tend to be overcooked. But here I have shortened the cooking time to preserve nutrients and texture.

Entrecote with Onion
(Entrecote con Sivoya)

Steak and onions is certainly one of the most international dishes in the Western world. Provided the meat is tender, this is a no-fail fast food.

½ yellow onion per person	1 entrecote per person
1 tablespoon light vegetable oil per serving	salt
	ground pepper

Peel and slice the onions thinly into rings

In a heavy skillet heat the oil, when it is piping hot put in the onion rings and saute them until they become deep brown in color. Remove and drain on a paper towel.

Saute the entrecotes in the same oil, or, if you prefer, grill them under the broiler.

Arrange them on a hot platter, top them with the sauteed onion rings. Add salt and a grinding of pepper to taste.

Turkish Beef Stew
(Tas Kebab)

Tas is the Turkish word for baking dish, and indicates that this "kebab" is not grilled on a spit, as may be expected, but prepared in an entirely different way. In this slowly cooking stovetop dish, the meat first absorbs the tasty juices of the wilting onions, vegetables and seasonings. And then the rice, added with additional cooking liquid, benefits from the happy combination.

2 pounds stewing beef, cubed	½ teaspoon pepper
3 tablespoons light vegetable oil	½ teaspoon sugar
2 onions, coarsely chopped	½ teaspoon cinnamon
3 red peppers, seeded and chopped	1½ cups beef broth or bouillon
4 ripe tomatoes, peeled, seeded and chopped	1 cup rice
1½ teaspoons salt	2 tablespoons chopped parsley

Cut the beef into 1-inch-thick cubes and set aside.

In a large, heavy, lidded pot or flameproof casserole, heat the oil and, uncovered, gently saute the onions and peppers, until they are soft. Add the tomatoes, the salt, pepper, sugar, cinnamon and ½ cup of the broth.

Add the cubed beef to the pan. Cook until the meat is barely tender, for about 1 hour. Add the remaining broth and bring to a boil. Add the rice and chopped parsley and mix well. Lower the heat, cover the pan with a clean kitchen towel and then top with the lid and cook over a low heat until the rice is cooked and the water is absorbed, about ½ hour.

Serves 6–8.

Balkan Beef Stew
(Guvetch con Karne)

A *guvetch*, to my knowledge, is the earthenware pot in which this potpourri of vegetables was baked. The dish can be made with vegetables alone, or with the addition of meat, as in this recipe, or fish (see p. 31). Without elegant trappings, it is a dish that will never let you down. In this large and varied array, every vegetable acts like a good neighbor — enhancing the flavors on its borders but never overpowering them. While an earthenware pot, with its slow, even heating, results in the best blend of tastes, other types of baking dishes can be substituted in a pinch.

2 pounds stewing beef
2 tablespoons light vegetable oil
2 onions, chopped coarsely
2 stalks celery, chopped coarsely
2 carrots, sliced
2 red peppers, seeded and sliced
2 green peppers, seeded and sliced
½ cup water
5 ripe tomatoes, peeled, seeded and chopped, or 1 large can tomato puree
3 zucchini, sliced (not peeled)

1 large eggplant, cubed (not peeled)
2 ounces stringbeans, sliced
2 ounces okra
2 ounces garden peas
1½ teaspoons salt
½ teaspoon pepper
1 teaspoon sugar
5 kernels allspice
3 large potatoes, peeled, cubed and parboiled for 5 minutes
3 tablespoons chopped dill

Cube the meat into 1-inch-thick cubes. In a heavy pot (lidded), heat the oil and saute the meat uncovered together with the chopped onions and chopped celery. Add the sliced carrots, the red and green peppers and a scant ½ cup water. Cover and cook for 10 minutes. Uncover. Add the peeled and chopped tomatoes (or the tomato puree), sliced zucchini, cubed eggplant, stringbeans, okra and peas. Mix together. Add the salt, ground pepper, sugar and allspice. Mix well again and cook for another 15 minutes.

Add the cubed and parboiled potatoes and mix into the meat-vegetable mixture. Spoon the entire mixture into an oiled open baking dish, sprinkle the chopped dill over it and bake in a 325° oven for 1½ hours or until a crust is formed. Serve immediately.

Serves 6–8.

Beef and Eggplant Stew
(Kvartikos di Mirindgena con Karne)

The subtle taste of the eggplant, bolstered by pepper and tomato define this beef stew as unmistakably Sephardic. It is lightly spiced, with only salt, sugar, and a small amount of parsley, but as the beef and vegetables cook slowly over a low heat their flavors join in a masterly blend of tastes.

1 pound stewing beef	1 large ripe tomato, peeled, seeded
2 large eggplants, unpeeled, cubed	and chopped
2 tablespoons vegetable oil	1 teaspoon salt
1 onion, coarsely chopped	1 cup water
1 sweet red pepper, seeded and	1 teaspoon sugar
chopped	2 tablespoons chopped parsley

Cube the stewing beef into 1-inch-thick cubes.

Sprinkle coarse salt over the cubed eggplant and drain. After ½ hour wash away the salt and drain again.

In a heavy (lidded) pot or flameproof casserole, heat the oil and saute, uncovered, the cubed meat together with the chopped onion. When the meat has browned, add the pepper, tomato, salt and ½ cup of the water. Cover and cook over a low heat for ½ hour.

Uncover, add the cubed eggplant, the sugar and the remaining ½ cup water. Cover again and continue to cook for another ½ hour over low heat, or until the meat is tender. Sprinkle the chopped parsley over and serve.

Serves 4–6.

Sauteed Cabbage with Beef
(Kol Dulce con Karne)

This dish has a slightly sweet-and-sour taste and a nice crust. One of its wonderful advantages is that it is prepared in stages — stage one on top of the stove, stage two in the oven — which can be readily separated for the convenience of the busy cook by anything from a few hours or a day or so. Reheated, its taste only improves.

3 tablespoons light vegetable oil
1 pound stewing beef, cubed into 1 inch cubes
1 yellow onion, chopped coarsely
1½ teaspoons salt
½ cup water
1 head cabbage, cut into quarters and sliced thinly

2 tomatoes, peeled, seeded and chopped or 2 tablespoons tomato paste
1 red pepper, seeded and chopped
½ teaspoon sugar
1 tablespoon sweet paprika
½ teaspoon pepper
bay leaf
juice of 1 lemon

In a heavy, lidded pot or flameproof casserole, heat the oil and saute together, uncovered, the cubed meat and the chopped onion. When the meat is brown, add 1 teaspoon of the salt and ½ cup water. Cover and cook over low heat for ½ hour. Add the cabbage, the tomatoes or tomato paste and red pepper. Add the remaining salt, the sugar, paprika, pepper, bay leaf and lemon juice. Continue cooking until meat is just tender, about 1 hour. Pour the stew into an oiled baking dish and bake uncovered in a 325° oven for another hour.

Serves 4–6.

Goulash with Egg Drops
(Goulash con Handrajos di Masa)

The difference between goulash and stew lies in the large quantity of onions required as well as in the obligatory paprika. In this version, a relatively small amount of liquid is added, so that the meat cooks in the juices released by the vegetables and is transformed by their flavors, especially those of the onions and peppers. The eggdrops served alongside, in place of the more usual rice, potatoes or noodles, add a light and pleasant touch.

2 pounds stewing beef	¾ cup water
2 tablespoons light vegetable oil	
3 pounds onions, chopped coarsely	**The Eggdrops:**
5 tomatoes, peeled, seeded and chopped coarsely	large pan of boiling salted water
	2 eggs, lightly beaten
2 red peppers, seeded and chopped coarsely	2 tablespoons flour
	1 tablespoon margarine, melted
1 teaspoon salt	1 tablespoon water
½ teaspoon sugar	½ teaspoon salt
2 tablespoons sweet paprika	¼ teaspoon pepper
bay leaf	

Cube the beef into 1-inch-thick cubes.

In a large, heavy, lidded pot or flameproof casserole, heat the oil, add the cubed meat and, uncovered, saute gently until the meat is brown. Remove with a slotted spoon and set aside. Saute the onions in the same oil. When they are soft, add the chopped tomatoes and chopped peppers and cook for 5 minutes. Return the meat to the casserole, add salt, sugar, paprika, bay leaf and ¼ cup water. Mix well, cover, cook over a low heat until meat is tender, about 1½ hours. Serve hot with eggdrops.

The Eggdrops
Have ready a large pan of boiling salted water. In a bowl beat eggs lightly and sprinkle in the flour. Mix in the flour and add the melted margarine, water, salt and pepper. Mix well, spoon small droplets of the batter into the boiling water and remove with a slotted spoon to a colander as they rise to the top. Prevent sticking together by brushing lightly with oil. Serve with goulash.

Serves 8.

Veal with Fruit
(Hamin Dulci)

On the rare occasions when we cooked meat with fruit, the fruit we used was usually quince, with its lovely tart flavor. Here, along with the sweet prunes and caramel syrup, they give the delicate veal a sweetish, full flavor.

2 pounds lean stewing veal	1 teaspoon salt
2 tablespoons light vegetable oil	1 pound prunes, pitted
3 quinces, unpeeled, quartered and cored	2 tablespoons sugar
½ cup water	1 tablespoon flour dissolved in 2 tablespoons water

Cut the meat into large 1½-inch cubes. In a heavy, lidded casserole, heat the oil and, uncovered, saute the meat. Remove the meat with a slotted spoon and set aside. Add the quinces to the casserole and cook until they are lightly browned. Return the meat to the casserole. Add ½ cup water and salt, cover and cook over a low heat for 20 minutes. Uncover, add the prunes and cook for another 10 minutes.

In another small pan melt the sugar. When it turns just brown, add the water in which you have dissolved the flour. Mix into the melted sugar and pour it all into the casserole. Cover and cook for another 15 minutes. Taste, correct the seasoning and serve with rice or potatoes.

Serves 6.

Veal Escallops with Lemon
(Sofrito di Bitela con Limon)

Plentiful quantities of lemon are used in the Sephardic kitchen — with vegetables, with fish, and often in tandem with veal. In this dish lemon and garlic create an elegant union to enhance the tender taste of the escallops. Serve with rice.

2 pounds veal escallops	½ cup water
2–3 tablespoons flour	juice of 1½ lemons
4 tablespoons light vegetable oil	ground white pepper
2 garlic cloves, chopped	2 tablespoons chopped parsley
1 teaspoon salt	

Dust the escallops with flour. In a heavy frying pan heat the oil and saute the escallops lightly on both sides. Add the chopped garlic, salt and ½ cup water. Cover and simmer for 15 minutes. Uncover, add lemon juice, some freshly ground pepper and the chopped parsley. Cover again and cook another 10 minutes. Serve immediately.

Serves 8.

Veal Paprikas
(Paprikas di Bitela)

Not quite a goulash, but a wonderful stew with peppers. Serve with rice or boiled potatoes.

2 pounds stewing veal, cubed into 1-inch cubes
2 tablespoons flour
2 tablespoons ground sweet paprika
3 tablespoons light vegetable oil
½ cup water
salt
2 onions, thinly sliced in rings

2 red peppers, seeded and sliced in rings
2 green peppers, seeded and sliced in rings
2 ripe tomatoes, peeled, seeded and chopped
½ teaspoon sugar
ground black pepper
3 tablespoons chopped parsley

Mix the flour and paprika on a flat plate and roll the meat into it, covering the meat all over and using all the mixture. In a heavy lidded casserole, heat half the oil and, uncovered, lightly saute the meat. Add ½ cup water, some salt, cover and cook gently for 15 minutes.

While the meat is cooking, saute the sliced onion and pepper rings in another frying pan, using the remaining oil. Add the tomatoes and cook for a few minutes. Add more salt and the sugar; spoon the vegetables over the meat in the casserole. Mix, cover and cook another ½ hour. Uncover, add ground black pepper and the chopped parsley before serving.

Serves 6–8.

Veal with Artichoke Hearts
(Articho con Bitela)

Veal and artichokes both have high priority in Sephardic cooking. Combined and liberally flavored with lemon, they make a delicate and luxurious stew. Serve on a bed of fluffy white rice.

12 artichokes	½ cup water
bowl of water	1 teaspoon salt
4 tablespoons flour	½ teaspoon sugar
juice of 2 lemons	ground pepper
2 pounds veal, cubed	2 tablespoons chopped parsley
2 tablespoons vegetable oil	

Remove the leaves and slice away the choke of the artichokes. Drop the hearts into a bowl of water into which have been dissolved 2 tablespoons flour and the juice of one lemon.

Cube the meat and dust lightly with the remaining 2 tablespoons of flour. In a deep, heavy, flameproof casserole with lid, heat the oil and saute the meat. Add the water and ½ teaspoon salt; cover and cook for 20 minutes. Uncover, add the artichoke hearts (if large, cut them in quarters), the remaining salt, sugar, ground pepper and the remaining lemon juice. Cover and cook over a low heat until meat is tender and artichokes done, about 1 hour. Uncover, add the chopped parsley and serve.

Serves 6–8.

Meat Patties
(Kjoftes di Karne)

The combination of ground beef and ground veal with chopped onion and pepper, minced parsley and dill, and cumin endows this large meat patty with the distinctive taste of the Sephardic kitchen.

1 pound ground lean beef
1 pound ground veal
2 slices white bread without crusts, soaked in water and squeezed dry
1 large onion, chopped finely
1 sweet red pepper, chopped finely
2 tablespoons chopped parsley
2 tablespoons chopped dill

1 tablespoon salt
1 teaspoon ground pepper
ground cumin (available on spice shelves)
2 tablespoons light vegetable oil
2 tablespoons water
2 eggs, lightly beaten

In a large bowl mix together the ground beef and ground veal. Crumble the squeezed-out bread over the meat, add the chopped onion, the red pepper, chopped parsley and dill, salt, pepper and cumin, oil, water and eggs. Mix and knead the mixture well. Shape into medium-sized, slightly flattened balls about 2 inches in diameter and fry in hot oil until crisp. Arrange on a paper towel to drain.

Makes about 25 patties.

Meatballs in Tomato Sauce
(Kjoftes di Karne in Sos di Domates)

Veal and beef together make a lighter meatball than beef alone. The meatballs and sauce are both gently seasoned, the predominant tastes being pepper — as much or as little as you want — and parsley. Serve over rice or vermicelli.

1 pound ground beef or ground veal or a mixture of both	**The Sauce:**
	⅓ cup tomato paste
1 slice bread soaked in water and squeezed dry	1 cup water
	1 stalk celery, whole
2 tablespoons water	3 sprigs parsley, whole
1 teaspoon salt	½ teaspoon salt
½ teaspoon pepper	¼ teaspoon sugar
2 tablespoons chopped parsley	½ teaspoon ground pepper
1 egg, lightly beaten	1 tablespoon chopped parsley
¼ cup oil for frying	

Put the meat into a bowl and crumble the squeezed-out bread on top. Mix and knead together. Add the water, salt, ground pepper, chopped parsley and the egg. Mix well again and form into small meatballs 1–1½ inches in diameter. Heat the oil in a skillet and fry the meatballs. Place them on a paper towel to drain.

The Sauce
In a casserole or saucepan with a lid, put the tomato paste, water, celery, parsley sprigs, salt and sugar. Cover and cook gently for 10 minutes. Uncover. Immerse the meatballs into the sauce and simmer for 15–20 minutes. Remove the celery and whole parsley sprigs and add ground pepper and chopped parsley. Serve over rice or vermicelli.

Serves 4.

Leek and Meat Pie
(Prasafucho)

This crustless pie, which comes out of the oven light, brown and crisp, was invariably dished up during Passover, and the whole preceding winter as well! Accented by a dash of lemon and accompanied by a leafy green salad, it makes a delightful luncheon meal.

3 pounds leeks, green tops removed	1 pound ground veal
large pan of salted water	1 teaspoon salt
2 onions, whole	½ teaspoon ground pepper
1 small celeriac (celery root), peeled	grinding of nutmeg
and whole	4 eggs
4 tablespoons light vegetable oil	lemon wedges

Heat the oven to 350°.

Wash the leeks carefully, and cut the white part into large 2- to 3-inch chunks. Bring a large pan of salted water to boil and add the leeks, the onions and celery root. Cook until all the vegetables are soft (about 30 minutes) and drain in a colander (you can save the water for a soup). When cool enough to handle, squeeze out all the excess moisture from the vegetables between the palms of your hands and chop finely.

In a heavy skillet, heat the oil and lightly saute the chopped vegetables until they are light golden in color. Set aside.

In a large bowl, mix the ground veal with the salt, ground pepper and a good grinding of nutmeg. Mix in the leek mixture well with the meat and blend in the eggs, one by one, beating lightly with each addition.

Spread the mixture on a round oiled 9-inch pie tin and bake in a preheated 350° oven for 45 minutes until puffed, brown and crisp. Serve with wedges of lemon.

Serves 6.

Meat-Filled Potato Burekas (Turnovers) (Burekas di Kartof)

These *burekas* actually consist of a ground beef mixture wrapped in a fine and light potato dough. They are made with ingredients readily at hand — potatoes, eggs, flour, and a bit of ground meat. And while their preparation takes some time, they are well worth it, especially when eaten hot, crisp and fresh.

2 pounds potatoes, peeled and quartered	½ pound ground lean beef
3 eggs	1 teaspoon salt
salt	½ teaspoon ground pepper
pepper	2 tablespoons chopped parsley
2 tablespoons flour, plus flour for dusting	½ cup water
	1 slice bread, crust removed, soaked in water and squeezed dry
1 small onion, chopped finely	1 egg white beaten
2 tablespoons vegetable oil	¼ cup oil for frying

Boil the peeled and quartered potatoes in salted water until they are soft. Drain, return the potatoes to the pan and shake over the heat until any excess moisture is gone.

Make a dough by mashing the potatoes in a bowl. Add 2 of the eggs, salt, ground pepper and 2 tablespoons flour.

In a small frying pan, lightly saute the chopped onion in 2 tablespoons oil, add the meat and cook until it just turns color. Add salt, ground pepper and chopped parsley and ½ cup water and cook for 15 minutes. Remove from heat and allow to cool. Crumble in the squeezed-out bread and add the remaining egg. Mix well.

Flour a board and roll or press out the potato dough to a ½-inch thickness. Cut 3-inch circles with a cutter or a glass. In the middle of each circle place a teaspoonful of the meat mixture. Gently fold over in half, press together and seal the edges with the beaten egg white. Fry in very hot oil. Drain on a paper towel and serve hot.

Makes about 15 *burekas*.

Baked Leg or Shoulder of Lamb
(Kodrero in Papel al Orno)

Wrapping the lamb in greaseproof paper — meaning waxed paper or aluminum foil — keeps in all of the meat's rich juices and ensures a tender and most flavorable dish. Wrap the lamb well so there are no leaks and season with lemon, rosemary and pepper.

leg or shoulder of lamb	½ teaspoon ground pepper
6–8 cloves garlic, peeled and sliced	1 teaspoon dried rosemary
into thin slivers	2 tablespoons vegetable oil
1 lemon, sliced in half	aluminum foil (or waxed paper)
1 teaspoon salt	

With a small, sharp knife, pierce the meat and insert the slivers of garlic into them. Rub the meat with the lemon, and season it with salt, ground pepper and rosemary. Rub the oil on the meat. Brush a large sheet of aluminum foil with more oil and wrap up the meat, making an airtight parcel. Place the wrapped-up leg on a roasting pan and cook in a 350° oven for 1½–2 hours depending on the size of the meat. Before serving, unwrap. The meat cooked this way retains all its juices and flavor.

Serves 6–8.

Lamp Chops with Spinach
(Kodrero con Spinaka)

We usually prepared lamb chops in either of two ways: quickly in the grill, or slowly in a skillet with vegetables and seasonings. In this slowly cooked version the slightly acerbic spinach absorbs the lamb's fatty juices and balances its rich flavor.

4 tablespoons light vegetable oil	½ cup water
1 small onion, chopped	3 pounds spinach
6 large lamb chops	juice of 1½ lemons
2 tablespoons flour	½ teaspoon sugar
1 teaspoon salt	½ teaspoon ground pepper

In a wide, heavy, flameproof casserole with lid, large enough to hold the chops in one layer, heat the oil and saute the onions, uncovered, until soft. Dust the lamb chops with the flour and add to the onions. Saute the chops on each side for a few minutes, add ½ teaspoon salt and the water, cover and cook for ½ hour.

Meantime, wash, chop and drain the spinach. After the meat has cooked for ½ hour, add the chopped spinach to the casserole. Add the lemon juice and sugar, cover and cook until the meat is tender. Uncover, add another ½ teaspoon of salt, a grinding of pepper and continue cooking uncovered for another 10–15 minutes, until all the water has evaporated.

Serves 6.

Lamb and Rice
(Kodrero con Aroz)

The Sephardic tradition of eating lamb as the main dish of the Passover Seder recalls the days before the destruction of the Second Temple when a one-year-old lamb was sacrificed on Passover eve and eaten the same night. Since Sephardic lore permits the use of rice during Passover, this baked lamb and rice dish was a traditional favorite at our Seder table.

4 pounds shoulder of lamb, cut into 1½-inch chunks	1 teaspoon salt
3 tablespoons olive oil	2 tablespoons chopped parsley
1 yellow onion, chopped coarsely	½ teaspoon ground pepper
3 cups water	2 cups rice

Cube the lamb into serving portions. In a deep, heavy casserole with lid, large enough to hold the lamb and finished rice, heat the oil and saute the chopped onion uncovered until light golden. Add the lamb and brown well on all sides. Add 1 cup water and ½ teaspoon salt; cover and simmer over low heat until the meat is almost tender, about 1 hour. Add enough water to measure 3 cups liquid, the chopped parsley, ground pepper and another ½ teaspoon salt. Bring the liquid to a boil and add the rice. Mix well with a wooden spoon, lower the heat, cover the pan with a clean kitchen towel, then top with the lid and cook over low heat until all liquid is absorbed and the rice is fluffy. Allow to rest 15 minutes before serving.

Serves 8–10.

Lamb with Fresh Onions and Garlic
(Kodrero con Ajo Fresco)

The arrival of new lamb coincided with the first crops of fresh garlic, and both were put together in this delicious combination. Find the garlic when it is still young and undivided into cloves. Use the head and part of the stem of the garlic.

¼ pound fresh (new) garlic with 2 inches of stalk	1–2 tablespoons flour
2 pounds spring onions, sliced in 2-inch lengths	2 tablespoons tomato paste
	2 tablespoons wine vinegar
4 tablespoons light vegetable oil	½ cup water
4 pounds shoulder or rack of lamb, cut into 1½-inch serving pieces	1½ teaspoons salt
	½ teaspoon sugar
	½ teaspoon ground pepper

Don't peel the garlic, simply snip off the root end. Slice, using the entire length of the stalk into two-inch lengths. Do the same with the green onion. Blanch both in boiling salted water for two minutes. Drain. Heat the oil in a deep, heavy, lidded casserole and saute the onions and garlic, uncovered, very lightly. Remove with slotted spoon and set aside.

Dust the lamb pieces with flour and saute in the same oil. Return the onions and garlic to the skillet, add the tomato paste, vinegar, water, salt, sugar and ground pepper and cook covered for half an hour. Place the covered skillet in a 350° oven for another half hour and then uncover for final 20 minutes cooking. Serve with *fideos* (p. 170) or rice.

Serves 8–10.

(Note: If the young garlic is unavailable, substitute 4 or 5 whole cloves of dried garlic. It's still good!)

Innard Pilaf
(Schlemelach)

It was not such a rarity back home to have a whole lamb delivered by the butcher. We usually took the opportunity to use the rich innards in this sumptious and variegated pilaf. It is not so easy to find all these parts, so in the spring, when young lambs appear, I call my butcher with an order for all the innards, and then invite my friends to a large buffet dinner where this is the all-in-one feature article.

sweetbreads, heart, lungs, kidneys and liver of baby lamb or veal, amounting to 3–4 pounds
2 pounds green onions, sliced into 1-inch lengths
4 tablespoons light vegetable oil

1½ teaspoons salt
ground pepper
2 tablespoons chopped parsley
2 tablespoons chopped dill
3 cups beef broth
2 cups rice

Soak the sweetbreads, heart and lungs in a bowl of cold water for half an hour. Drain and put them into a saucepan together with the kidneys. Cover with cold water, bring to a boil and parboil for 10 minutes. Drain and cube each meat into ½-inch cubes. Set aside.

In a heavy, lidded large casserole, large enough for the finished dish, heat the oil and lightly fry the sliced green onion. Add the cubed sweetbreads, heart, kidneys and lungs. Mix well, lower the flame and cook for 15 minutes.

Broil the liver, on both sides, and rinse. Cube the liver and add it to the casserole. Add salt, ground pepper, chopped parsley and dill and the 3 cups of beef broth. Mix well and bring to a boil. Add the rice, mix well with a wooden spoon, bring again to a boil, lower the heat, cover the pan with a clean towel, then with its lid and cook for about 20–30 minutes or until rice is cooked and all the water has been absorbed. Allow to rest 5 minutes before serving.

Serves 10–12.

Tongue with Garlic
(Luenga con Ajo)

Tongue, an absorbent and rather bland meat on its own, always benefits from the proximity of strong spices. Hence the four to five heads of garlic in this recipe. The final taste, however, has nothing of the sharpness you might expect. With the skin kept on, the garlic becomes creamy and mellow. Garlic is actually quite an unusual spice: when massive quantities are cooked slowly, the taste acquires considerable subtlety and the numerous garlic cloves endow the dish with a substantial texture and rich aroma.

1 beef tongue, fresh	1 whole carrot, scraped
2 tablespoons light vegetable oil	1 leek, whole
4–5 entire heads of garlic, separated but unpeeled	1 celery stalk, whole
	1 teaspoon salt
1 tablespoon flour	1 bay leaf
1 cup water	5 pepper kernels

Wash the tongue thoroughly, and soak in cold water for an hour. Blanch the tongue in boiling salted water for ½ hour. Drain and peel off the skin. In a large, heavy casserole, heat the oil, add all the garlic cloves and saute them lightly. Sprinkle with flour, add 1 cup water and bring to a boil. Add the peeled tongue, carrot, leek, celery stalk, salt, bay leaf, pepper kernels; cover and cook until tongue is tender, about 1 hour.

Before serving, slice the tongue and arrange on a deep serving dish. Surround with the garlic cloves, removed with a slotted spoon from sauce. Strain the sauce and pour over the sliced tongue.

Serves 6.

Tongue with Black Olives
(Luenga con Azei Tunas)

Boiled tongue is peeled, sliced and arranged in a flavorful tomato sauce perked up with lemon juice, salt, sugar and cinnamon, and plenty of black olives. It can be served hot or at room temperature, so it makes a convenient party dish.

2 cups water	1 tablespoon flour dissolved in ½ cup water
1 tablespoon salt	
6 peppercorns	juice of ½ lemon
1 yellow onion, peeled and whole	½ teaspoon salt
1 leek, sliced in 2-inch lengths	½ teaspoon sugar
1 carrot, whole	1 teaspoon sugar
1 celery stalk, whole	1 teaspoon cinnamon
1 fresh beef tongue	20 black olives, pitted
2 tablespoons oil	½ teaspoon ground pepper
1 cup tomato puree	

In a large iron casserole, put 2 cups of water with 1 tablespoon salt, the peppercorns, peeled onion, leek slices, carrot and celery. Immerse the tongue. Bring to a boil and cook over a low heat until the tongue is tender. Allow to cool in the cooking liquid. Remove the tongue, peel and slice.

In a large frying pan, heat the oil, add the tomato puree, the flour dissolved in ½ cup water, the lemon juice, salt, sugar and cinnamon and cook for 5 minutes. Add the pitted olives, the tongue slices and the pepper to the sauce. Cook gently for 10 minutes before serving.

Serves 6.

POULTRY

Poultry

Among our people poultry was more widely eaten than beef and was even considered a finer delicacy.

The variety of dishes was endless. In addition to being roasted in the oven, poultry was pot roasted on top of the stove; often it was cut up, browned in oil and simmered with vegetables. I give recipes here for chicken with okra, olives, green peas, onions, quince, rice, potatoes and mixed vegetables, for turkey with rice and with cabbage, and for duck with sauerkraut. But really there is no end to the possible combinations and an imaginative cook can come up with the most unexpected variations.

Most of these dishes are uncomplicated and quick to make, inventive rather than extravagant. The vegetables keep the poultry moist and succulent; the poultry flavors the vegetables; and each combination produces its own unique blend of tastes.

Another common way we had of preparing chicken was to grind up the tender white meat of the breast, mix in spices and shape it into small balls to be fried in hot oil or cooked in a tasty sauce. Here, too, the possible combinations are endless, while the particular spice and sauce give each version its special dimension.

Chicken with Garden Peas
(Pojo con Bizelias)

Since their discovery at the end of the 17th century, peas have been considered a great delicacy. And they still are. Enhanced with dill and a pinch of sugar, they give this chicken dish a sweet garden flavor and a lovely spring appearance. If you use frozen peas, don't precook them.

2 young chickens, cut into serving pieces	2 pounds fresh garden peas (weigh shelled) or, if not available, 2 10- oz. packages frozen peas
salt	
3–4 tablespoons flour	½ teaspoon sugar
2 tablespoons light vegetable oil	½ teaspoon pepper
½ cup water	2 tablespoons chopped dill
2 stalks celery, whole with leaves	

Salt the chicken parts and dust them with flour. In a heavy (lidded) skillet or flameproof casserole, heat the oil and saute the chicken pieces until lightly golden. Add ½ cup water, cover and cook over a low flame for 20 minutes.

Uncover, add the celery (whole) and the peas. Cover and cook for a further 20 minutes. Uncover, add the sugar, ground pepper and chopped dill. Cook another 5 minutes, arrange the chicken on a serving platter, and pour the sauce over, with or without the celery.

Serves 6–8.

Chicken with Okra
(Pojo con Bambya)

This dish asks for the tiniest okra you can find. The vegetable's season is short and worth taking advantage of. Though frozen okra can be used, I personally don't. Serve with boiled rice to soak up the thick, savory sauce.

2 pounds okra, stemmed
water to cover, acidulated with 2 tablespoons vinegar
2 tablespoons light vegetable oil
2 young chickens, cut into serving pieces
1 small onion, chopped coarsely

6 ripe tomatoes, peeled, seeded and chopped
¾ cup water
1 teaspoon salt
½ teaspoon pepper
½ teaspoon sugar
⅓ cup dry red wine

Clean the okra, removing the stems, and cover with water mixed with the vinegar. Allow to stand for ½ hour and drain.

In a heavy lidded skillet, large enough to hold both chicken and vegetables, heat the oil, add the pieces of chicken and chopped onion and saute together for a few minutes. Add the tomatoes, the water, salt, pepper and sugar. Cover and cook for 20–25 minutes. Uncover, add the okra and wine. Cover and cook for another 20–25 minutes, or until done. Taste, correct seasoning, add another grind of pepper and serve.

Serves 6–8.

Chicken with Olives
(Pojo con Azeitunas)

All of our chicken dishes have one thing in common: you start by searing the pieces in oil, continue cooking with a small amount of liquid, add the vegetables midway, and finish off with the last spices. As overcooked olives have a tendency to toughen, it's a good idea to add them only when reheating if you prepare the dish in advance.

2 tablespoons oil	1 teaspoon salt
1 medium-sized chicken, cut into serving pieces	½ teaspoon sugar
	1 garlic clove, crushed
4 tomatoes, peeled, seeded and chopped, or, if not available,	⅓ cup red wine
	20 pitted black olives, blanched for 1 minute in boiling water
2 tablespoons tomato paste	
1 tablespoon flour, dissolved in 2 tablespoons water	3 tablespoons chopped parsley
	grinding of pepper

In a heavy (lidded) skillet, or flameproof casserole, heat the oil and saute the chicken. Remove the chicken and set aside.

In the same oil, cook the chopped tomatoes (if you are using tomato paste add that). Dissolve the flour in 2 tablespoons water and add to the pan. Add the salt, sugar, crushed garlic and the wine. Mix well.

Return the pieces of chicken to the pan, cover and cook over a low heat for 25 minutes.

Uncover, add the pitted, blanched olives and chopped parsley. Mix, cover and cook for another 10 minutes. Before serving, add a grinding of pepper. Serve with noodles.

Serves 4–6.

Chicken with Onions
(Armi di Gaina)

Positively smothered in onions set off by sweet red peppers, nutty allspice and paprika, this chicken dish has a sultry mellow flavor. I recommend serving it with rice or simple boiled potatoes to gather up the last drops of the delicious sauce.

3 tablespoons light vegetable oil	2 tablespoons sweet paprika
1 large chicken, cut into 6–8 serving pieces	bay leaf
3 pounds onions, sliced thinly	10 peppercorns
2 red peppers, seeded and sliced	5 allspice kernels
1 teaspoon salt	½ cup water
	ground pepper

In a heavy, lidded skillet or flameproof casserole, heat the oil and saute the chicken pieces lightly, until they are slightly golden. Remove the chicken with a slotted spoon and set aside.

In the same oil cook the onions and peppers until the onions turn golden and the peppers soften. Replace the chicken pieces on the bed of onions and peppers, sprinkle with salt and paprika. Add the bay leaf, peppercorns and allspice, tied into a piece of cheesecloth. Pour in in ½ cup of water, cover and cook until the chicken is tender, about 30–40 minutes. Uncover, add a grinding of pepper. Taste, correct the seasoning and serve with rice and pickled vegetables.

Serves 6–8.

Chicken with Glazed Baby Onions (Pojo con Arpadjic)

The glazed onions give this dish a caramel taste and rich brown color. The small fresh onions about one inch in diameter and available at the end of the summer are best. For the rest of the year you can use frozen baby onions. Only be careful to shake them gently so that they don't fall apart, and reduce the cooking time at the end from 15 to 10 minutes.

1 medium roasting chicken, or 6–8 pieces chicken parts	2 pounds small onions, peeled
3 tablespoons light vegetable oil	2–3 tablespoons sugar
1 teaspoon salt	juice of 1 lemon
1¼ cups water	freshly ground pepper

Wash and cut up the chicken into 8 pieces. In a heavy, lidded skillet or a flameproof casserole, heat 2 tablespoons of the oil and brown the chicken on all sides.

When the chicken is nicely colored, add salt and ¾ cup water, and cook over a low heat, covered, for 20 minutes.

While the chicken is cooking, blanch the onions for 1 minute in boiling water. Drain. In a separate skillet, melt the sugar in the remaining tablespoon of oil until just light brown. Add the onions and shake the pan until the onions are nicely glazed.

Add the onions with their glaze to the chicken, mixing in gently in order not to break up the small onions. Add another ½ cup of water, cover again and cook for another 15 minutes.

Uncover, add the lemon juice and a grinding of black pepper; taste the sauce for seasoning and serve.

Serves 6–8.

Chicken with Vegetables
(Gaina con Zarzavat)

A simple dish worthy of an epicurean palate. The steam from the vegetables rises to enhance the flavor of the chicken, while the luscious chicken juices seep down into the fresh vegetables. For best results, remove whatever fat may be on the chicken.

3 tablespoons light vegetable oil
1 large chicken, cut into serving pieces
1 onion, chopped coarsely
2 red peppers, seeded, and sliced in rings
2 green peppers, seeded and sliced into rings
2 stalks celery, chopped

4 ripe tomatoes, peeled, seeded and sliced
2 cloves garlic, crushed
1 teaspoon salt
¼ teaspoon sugar
½ cup water
3 tablespoons chopped dill
freshly ground pepper

In a heavy (lidded) skillet or flameproof casserole, heat the oil and saute the chicken pieces lightly. Remove with a slotted spoon and set aside. Add to the same oil the chopped onion, the peppers, celery, tomatoes and crushed garlic. Cook for a few minutes, until the vegetables soften, and add the salt and sugar.

Arrange the pieces of chicken on the vegetable bed. Add ½ cup water, cover and simmer until tender, about 30–40 minutes.

When ready, arrange on a serving dish, sprinkle with chopped dill, grind over some pepper, and serve with boiled potatoes or rice, with pickled vegetables alongside.

Serves 6–8.

Chicken and Rice
(Gaina con Aroz)

No Friday night dinner or Saturday lunch went by without the traditional chicken and rice. They were cooked together in a savory stock that had been flavored with the traditional soup vegetables and accented with cinnamon and grated lemon rind to create a subtle, most agreeable blend of tastes. In winter we had it accompanied by beetroot salad or pickles, in summer by grilled peppers.

2 tablespoons light vegetable oil	1 cup water
6–8 pieces chicken	1 teaspoon salt
1 onion, peeled and whole	½ teaspoon pepper
1 carrot, whole	1½ cups rice
1 bay leaf	grated rind of ½ lemon
1 stalk celery, with leaves	½ teaspoon cinnamon
3 sprigs parsley	2 tablespoons chopped parsley

Your cooking pot should be large enough to hold both chicken and finished rice.

In a large, lidded skillet or flameproof casserole, heat the oil and saute the chicken parts lightly on all sides. Add onion, carrot, bay leaf, celery stalk and parsley. Pour in 1 cup of water and the salt and pepper, cover and cook on a low heat for 20 minutes.

Remove the chicken from the pan, strain the stock, measure it and add enough water to make 2½ cups liquid. Reserve.

Replace the chicken pieces in the pan. Sprinkle in the rice, the grated lemon peel and the cinnamon, and pour the chicken stock over it all. Cover, bring to a boil, lower the heat and cook slowly until all water is absorbed and the rice is cooked, about 15 minutes. Uncover, add another grinding of fresh pepper, sprinkle with fresh parsley and cover the pan with a clean towel. Allow to stand for 15 minutes before serving. Serve with pickled vegetables.

Serves 6–8.

Chicken and Potatoes
(Gaina con Kartof)

The sliced red peppers add zest and an almost herblike flavor to this basic chicken and potato dish, and bring a cheering dash of color to the table.

3 tablespoons light vegetable oil	1 teaspoon salt
1 large chicken, cut into serving pieces	1 cup water
1 large onion, chopped	6 large potatoes, peeled and quartered
2 red peppers, seeded and sliced into rings	ground pepper
	2 tablespoons chopped parsley

In a heavy skillet, with lid, or a flameproof casserole, heat the oil and saute the pieces of chicken lightly. Remove the chicken with a slotted spoon and set aside.

In the same oil, saute the onions and red peppers until soft. Return the chicken to the pan, add the salt and ½ cup of the water. Cover and cook over a low heat for 15 minutes.

Uncover, add another ½ cup of water and the quartered potatoes. Bring the water to a boil, lower the heat, cover and cook slowly until the water is absorbed and the potatoes cooked, approximately 20 minutes.

Arrange the chicken and potatoes on a serving platter, grind over some pepper, pour the pan juices over and sprinkle with chopped parsley. Serve with a variety of pickled vegetables.

Serves 6.

Chicken with Quince
(Pojo con Binbriyo)

In the Middle Ages meat and fruit were commonly cooked together. Then, as tastes changed, the combination practically disappeared, and in Bulgaria at least they were seldom joined. This chicken and quince dish is one of the rare exceptions.

2 tablespoons light vegetable oil	½ teaspoon salt
2 young chickens, cut into serving pieces	2 tablespoons sugar
	½ cup water
2 pounds fresh quince, unpeeled, cored and quartered	1 tablespoon flour

In a heavy, lidded skillet or flameproof casserole, heat the oil and saute the chicken lightly. With a slotted spoon remove the pieces to a warm oven.

In the same oil, saute the quince quarters. Return the chicken to the pan, together with its juices. Salt lightly, cover and continue to cook gently for 25 minutes.

In a second skillet, cook the sugar until light brown, add the water mixed with flour, and cook for 2 minutes. Pour the sauce over the chicken and quince, and finish cooking in a 350° oven for another 15 minutes.

Serves 6–8.

Chicken Breast Meatballs with Garlic (Albondigas con Ajo)

In large quantities, garlic gives off a rich, full-bodied flavor, entirely unlike the expected taste. And it has the further attribute of thickening the sauce without flour. You can use fresh or frozen garlic. Serve with the Italian fettucini or tagliatelli if you can get them, and if not, with fine or medium noodles.

2 tablespoons water	3 tablespoons chopped dill
4 tablespoons flour	2 tablespoons light vegetable oil
1 pound ground chicken breast	10 cloves garlic, peeled and halved
1 teaspoon salt	1 cup water
½ teaspoon white pepper	½ lemon
½ teaspoon nutmeg	

In a small bowl mix 2 tablespoons water with 2 tablespoons of the flour. Add ground breast of chicken, salt, ground pepper, nutmeg and 1 tablespoon of the dill. Mix well.

In a lidded deep skillet or flameproof casserole large enough to hold the meatballs, heat the oil and saute the garlic until light golden. Sprinkle in the remaining 2 tablespoons of flour. Stir well and add the cup of water, salt and more ground pepper. Allow to boil, lower the heat and cook for a few minutes.

Shape the meat mixture into small balls (1 inch in diameter) and add to the saucepan. Cover and cook over a low heat for ½ hour. Uncover, add squeeze of lemon juice and the remaining chopped dill, taste, rectify seasoning and serve.

Serves 4; more as part of buffet.

Chicken Breast Meatballs with Garlic and Potatoes
(Albondigas con Kartofis i Ajo)

Whenever I think about this dish, I remember the wonderful aroma of garlic that filled our kitchen whenever Mother prepared it. Robust and filling, these saucy little meatballs were perfect on a cold winter night.

2 tablespoons flour
2 cups water
1 pound ground chicken breast
3 tablespoons light vegetable oil
1½ teaspoons salt
½ teaspoon pepper
6 cloves garlic, coarsely chopped

¾ cup tomato paste
1 celery stalk, finely chopped
6 medium potatoes, peeled and quartered
½ teaspoon white pepper
2 tablespoons chopped parsley

In a mixing bowl, blend the flour into ½ cup of the water. Add the ground chicken, 1 tablespoon of the oil, half a teaspoon of the salt and the ground pepper. Knead the mixture well. Form into small meatballs, not more than one inch in diameter.

In a heavy, deep lidded skillet or flameproof casserole, heat the remaining oil and add the chopped garlic. Cook for a minute and add the tomato paste, 1 cup of the water, the remaining teaspoon of salt and the chopped celery. Bring to a boil, cover the skillet, lower the heat and cook gently for 10 minutes. Uncover and add the meatballs and the quartered potatoes to the sauce and the remaining ½ cup water. Cover and cook until the potatoes are soft, about half an hour. Uncover, add the ground pepper and the chopped parsley.

Serves 6.

Small Chicken Breast Meatballs in Lemon Sauce
(Albondigas con Limon)

This is almost an adaptation of the Greek method of cooking vegetables. Poached in a mixture of lemon and oil, the little chicken balls acquire an intriguing tangy taste, which is best complemented by a generous serving of rice. I especially enjoy it in summer.

2 tablespoons flour	2 tablespoons light vegetable oil
2 tablespoons water	1 cup water
1 pound chicken breast, ground	juice of 1½ lemons
1 teaspoon salt	½ teaspoon salt
½ teaspoon pepper	½ teaspoon sugar
1 teaspoon nutmeg	freshly ground pepper
3 tablespoons chopped dill	

In a small bowl mix the flour and water, add the ground chicken, salt, pepper, nutmeg and 1 tablespoon of chopped dill. Mix well and form into small balls (1 inch diameter)

In a saucepan with lid or flameproof casserole large enough to hold all the meatballs bring to a boil the oil, 1 cup water, lemon juice, the remaining 2 tablespoons chopped dill, salt and sugar. Cook for 10 minutes.

Immerse the meatballs into the saucepan, cover and cook gently for 20–25 minutes. Remove from heat and add a good grinding of pepper. Serve on a bed of rice or noodles.

Serves 4.

Chicken Breast Rissoles
(Fritakas di Karne Blanca de Gaina)

These chicken breast patties were a Passover staple. Matza soaked in water replaced the bread.

1½ pounds ground breast of chicken
1 slice bread without crust, soaked and squeezed
1 small onion, grated
1 tablespoon light vegetable oil
2 tablespoons water

2 tablespoons chopped dill
1 teaspoon salt
½ teaspoon pepper
¼ teaspoon nutmeg
2 eggs, lightly beaten
frying oil

Work the squeezed-out bread into the ground chicken breast. Add the grated onion, oil, 2 tablespoons water, chopped dill, salt, ground pepper, nutmeg, beaten eggs and mix well. Shape into patties and fry in hot oil. Serve with *agristada* or Passover mayonnaise.

Makes about 30 rissoles.

Boiled Mayonnaise
(Agristada)

Don't be misled by the word *mayonnaise* in the title. Though it has the tang of mayonnaise and the texture of a chilled white sauce, *agristada* is a dish in its own right. It can be served quite successfully with only a crunchy chunk of white bread. And when it is brought to the table as an accompaniment to boiled fish, chicken breasts, or brains it is the *agristada* that provides the dominant flavor.

4 eggs	1 teaspoon salt
4 teaspoons flour	2 teaspoons sugar
2 cups water	juice of 1½ lemons
¼ cup light vegetable oil	parsley

Break the eggs into a small enamel saucepan and beat them lightly with a fork. Put the flour into a small bowl and add ½ cup of the water, mixing continually to dissolve the flour. Add the flour-water mixture to the eggs, mixing well. Whisk in the remaining water, the oil, salt, sugar and lemon juice. Place the pan on a low heat. Whisk all the while, or stir continually with a wooden spoon, until the mixture thickens and comes to a boil. Remove from heat, continue to stir for another minute, pour into a serving dish, and cover to prevent a film from forming. Chill.

You can store the *agristada* for several days in the refrigerator.

This *agristada* can be served with cold fish, brains or white poultry meat.

Just before serving, fry some coarsely chopped parsley in a little oil, and pour the oil over the chilled *agristada*.

Yield: 2½ cups *agristada*.

Accompaniment for 6.

Mock Brains
(Miyoyo Falso)

This dish, traditionally made with sour green plums, was always a favorite with children — who greedily consumed the uncooked fruit before it had a chance to reach its destination. If you can't get the green plums, lemon juice makes a satisfactory substitute. Cooked in the citric juices, the chicken balls attain the soft texture of brains — hence the name.

3 tablespoons light vegetable oil	1 teaspoon salt
2 tablespoons chopped dill	½ teaspoon sugar
3 tablespoons flour	2 tablespoons water
1 cup water	1 pound ground breast of chicken
½ pound green plums (pitted and chopped) or, if unavailable, the juice of 1½ lemons	½ teaspoon white pepper
	½ teaspoon ground nutmeg
	2 eggs

In a deep, heavy lidded skillet or flameproof casserole heat the oil and saute 1 tablespoon of the chopped dill, for a minute. Sprinkle in 1 tablespoon of the flour, whisk into the oil, and slowly add the cup of water, mixing it into the flour and oil, continue to stir making sure there are no lumps. Add the plums (or lemon juice), ½ teaspoon of salt and a pinch of sugar. Bring to a boil and cook slowly for 15 minutes.

In a bowl mix the remaining flour and 2 tablespoons water, add the ground meat, another ½ teaspoon of salt, ground pepper, nutmeg and the remaining chopped dill. Mix well and shape into small patties. Immerse the patties into the sauce, cover and cook for 15 minutes.

In a small bowl beat the two eggs lightly and pour into them a ladleful of the sauce. Mix and return the egg mixture to the saucepan, stirring it with a wooden spoon.

Let it thicken. but not boil. Serve immediately.

Serves 4.

Braised Capon
(Gaina Abafada)

This was our traditional way of serving a whole chicken. Cooked on top of the stove it retained all of its juicy, succulent flavor. To best enjoy its pure simplicity, season with a light hand.

1 large capon, or roasting chicken	2 tablespoons light vegetable oil
salt	1 carrot, whole
½ lemon	1 onion, whole
2 stalks celery with their leaves	½ cup water
3 sprigs parsley, with stems	ground pepper

Wash and dry the chicken, rub the inside with salt and the ½ lemon. Insert the celery stalks and parsley sprigs into the chicken.

In a large, deep, lidded skillet or dutch oven, heat the oil and saute the chicken slowly on all sides until it becomes a nice golden color. Add the carrot and onion. Sprinkle some salt over the chicken, add ½ cup water, cover and cook on a very low heat for ¾ hour or until the chicken is tender. Remove the chicken to a warm serving platter. Strain the sauce, add some ground pepper and serve separately as sauce for accompanying rice or mashed potatoes.

Serves 6.

Jellied Cockerel
(Gaylo Ilado)

This cold dish always required a young rooster in our house, because grandmother insisted that only its glutinous comb could make the aspic jell properly. But today you can use a lean fryer.

1 young cockerel or young chicken
rind and juice of 1 lemon
2 carrots, sliced
1 onion, whole
2 celery stalks, whole
3 parsley sprigs
1 teaspoon salt

10 peppercorns
water to cover
1 pickled cucumber
parsley, for garnish
½ teaspoon sugar
ground white pepper

Clean and wash the cockerel. Skin the lemon and blanch the pieces of rind.

In a large, deep lidded pot or a dutch oven, put the carrots, onion, celery, sprigs of parsley, lemon rind, salt, peppercorns and, on top, the cockerel. Cover with water, bring to a boil, cover, lower the heat and simmer for ¾ hour until tender. Allow the bird to cool in the cooking liquid. When cool, but not chilled, remove the cockerel from the saucepan. Remove the skin and bones from the cockerel, and arrange the pieces of meat on a serving dish, decorating them with the sliced carrots, some fresh parsley and slices of pickled cucumbers.

Strain the cooking liquid through a wet cheesecloth, and return to the pan. Cook over high heat until reduced to half its original volume. Add the lemon juice and sugar and pour over the cockerel. Add a grinding of white pepper, cool and place in refrigerator until it jells; at least 3 hours.

Serves 4.

Turkey Drumsticks and Cabbage
(Biba con Kol Dulce)

Smothered in cabbage, the turkey remains moist and juice. They are pre-cooked separately and then baked together until the flavors are well blended and the spices — allspice and cumin — have been well absorbed.

4 tablespoons vegetable oil	1 bay leaf
8–10 turkey drumsticks, or other parts	5 allspice kernels
	½ teaspoon ground cumin
1 teaspoon salt in ¾ cup water	1 teaspoon salt
1 onion, chopped coarsely	¼ teaspoon sugar
1 head cabbage, shredded	juice of 1 lemon
1 red pepper, seeded and chopped	¼ cup water
1 or 2 tart apples, peeled, cored and sliced	ground pepper
	1 tablespoon sweet paprika

In a heavy, lidded skillet or flameproof casserole, heat half the oil and saute the pieces of turkey until they are light brown. Add salt, ¾ cup water and cook slowly about ¾ hour.

While the turkey is cooking, in another large, lidded skillet, heat the remaining oil and saute the chopped onion, the shredded cabbage and chopped pepper. Cook the mixture for 3–4 minutes, mixing it well with a wooden spoon.

To the vegetables add the apples, bay leaf, allspice, ground cumin, salt, sugar and the lemon juice. Add the ¼ cup water, cover and cook over a low heat. After 30 minutes uncover, and add a grinding of black pepper.

In an oiled baking dish large enough to hold everything, arrange pieces of turkey. Spoon the vegetables in and around the pieces of turkey and pour over the liquid in which the pieces of turkey have been cooked. Sprinkle generously with sweet paprika. Bake in a 350° oven for another hour or until the cabbage has formed a crust.

Serves 8–10.

Sweet and Sour Turkey with Rice
(Biba con Kol Agra i Aroz)

Our homemade pickled cabbage came in handy for this dish. My mother would go down to the cellar, remove a pickled cabbage from the barrel, and proceed from there. Today, canned sauerkraut supplies the punch and pungency. Especialy fitting for a hearty winter meal.

4 tablespoons oil	1 bay leaf
6 turkey legs, or other parts, or a mixture	10 kernels allspice
	1 teaspoon sugar
1 teaspoon salt	2 teaspoons sweet paprika
1 cup water	½ teaspoon pepper
2 large cans sauerkraut	1 cup rice
1 onion, chopped	1¼ cups water
3–4 tablespoons oil	paprika for top

In a very large lidded skillet, or flameproof casserole, heat half the oil and brown the pieces of turkey well. Add salt, and one cup of water, cover and cook until almost done, about ¾ hour.

Wash and drain the sauerkraut. Heat the remaining oil in a saucepan, add the sauerkraut and onion and fry over a low heat for about 5 minutes, mixing it all the while with a large wooden spoon.

Add the bay leaf, the allspice, sugar, paprika, the grinding of pepper and the rice. Mix well, add 1¼ cups water. Bring to a boil. Cover, lower the heat and cook for 15 minutes until the rice has absorbed the water. Remove from heat.

In an oiled baking dish, arrange the pieces of turkey. Spoon the cabbage-rice around them. Pour the juice remaining from both skillets over the turkey, sprinkle more paprika on top and bake in a 350° oven for ¾ hour, until a crust is formed.

Serves 6.

Duckling with Sauerkraut
(Patu con Kol Agra)

A duckling is a domesticated duck that has spent seven or eight weeks of its life on a farm before reaching your butcher. The sauerkraut cuts the bird's natural fattiness and the sweet paprika adds a delicate flavor all its own.

2 tablespoons vegetable oil	1 bay leaf
1 duckling, cut into 6 serving pieces	10 peppercorns
1 teaspoon salt	¼ teaspoon sugar
¾ cups water	2 tablespoons paprika
2 cans sauerkraut	¼ cup water

In a heavy lidded skillet or flameproof casserole, heat the oil and saute lightly the pieces of duckling. Add salt, ¾ cup of water and cook covered until half done, about 30 minutes. Remove the pieces of duck with a slotted spoon and set aside.

Wash the sauerkraut and drain. Add to the same skillet, and cook for 7–8 minutes, mixing it well with a wooden spoon. Add the bay leaf, peppercorns, sugar and paprika.

In an oiled baking dish arrange the pieces of duckling, surround with the sauerkraut. Add ¼ cup water to the juices in the skillet and pour over the duckling. Bake in a medium oven for 1 hour or until the duck is crisp.

Serves 4–6.

MEAT-STUFFED VEGETABLES, MOUSSAKAS AND PATTIES

Meat-stuffed Vegetables, Moussakas and Patties

In the Sephardic kitchen we often combine ground meat and vegetables in one form or another. The vegetables tend to tenderize the meat, the meat perks up the flavor of the vegetables. Each way of combining, through stuffing, stewing or braising together, layering in moussakas, or mixing in patties, yields its own particular texture and taste, and within the groups each individual combination has its own special charm. I have given here particular combinations, but obviously the partners can be changed and rechanged, as in an old-fashioned circle dance, always with interesting results.

What vegetables can be stuffed? Almost all of them. Any, in fact, big enough to cut open, remove the pulp or seeds, and put a bit of ground meat into or with leaves sturdy enough to serve as wrapping. Peppers, tomatoes, zucchini, eggplant, artichokes, grape leaves, cabbage and even chard — to name only those that I have given recipes for. The preparation of course involves several steps but is generally not difficult, and once you get the knack goes quite quickly. These dishes, in particular, lend themselves to many occasions, from a simple family meal to an elegant party or buffet.

Moussaka is a name you probably associate with an eggplant, meat and tomato casserole. But for us, eggplant moussaka is only one of very many kinds. For the word is actually a generic term that refers to any baked dish where meat and vegetables are arranged in alternating layers, bound together by a sauce, and baked in the oven. So we also have zucchini moussaka and potato moussaka — and if you let your imagination roam you can undoubtedly invent others.

Our patties are usually made with potatoes, spinach, eggplant, zucchini and leeks, all of which blend superbly with ground beef. Somehow, I remember that there were always plenty of these delicacies being prepared in our kitchen — meat being ground, vegetables precooked and mashed, and the whole mixed, seasoned, fried in hot oil until they had a nice crisp surface. Sometimes they were finished off in a rich chicken broth, making them extraordinarily soft and mellow. Inevitably they were eaten more quickly than they were made, and no matter what quantities were brought to the table, there were seldom leftovers.

Stuffed Red Tomatoes
(Domates Kolrados Inchidos con Karne)

It's impossible to imagine Sephardic cooking without the versatile tomato. One of the nicest uses I know is as casing for a meat and rice stuffing. Be sure to choose large, ripe and very firm tomatoes, and to drain them well after you remove the pulp, as excess juices will make the dish watery. Served on a platter with stuffed peppers and zucchini, they make a colorful addition to a buffet.

12 large, round, firm tomatoes	**The sauce:**
1 pound chopped lean beef	2 tablespoons vegetable oil
1 large onion, chopped finely	1 cup light tomato puree
¼ cup rice	1 cup water
1 teaspoon salt	juice of ½ lemon
½ teaspoon pepper	1 tablespoon sugar
3 tablespoons chopped parsley	2 stalks celery, chopped coarsely with leaves
	salt
	pepper

Wash and cut off one-quarter from the top of each tomato. Remove the inedible crown from the top quarter and chop the remaining part. Scoop out the bottom part of each tomato and remove as many of the seeds as possible. Chop the pulp and reserve with the chopped tops. Turn each tomato upside down to drain.

In a large mixing bowl, mix the ground meat with the chopped onion, raw rice, salt, pepper and chopped parsley. Add the chopped tomato and mix well. Stuff the drained tomatoes three-quarters full with the meat-rice mixture. Arrange them upright in a baking dish large enough to hold all the tomatoes on one level.

In a saucepan heat the oil, add the tomato puree, the water, the lemon juice, sugar and celery stalks. Cook over a low heat for 10 minutes. Taste and correct seasoning, adding salt and ground pepper.

Pour the sauce over the tomatoes in the baking dish, inserting the celery pieces between the tomatoes, cover with aluminum foil and bake in a 350° oven for 30–40 minutes. Uncover and cook for another 15 minutes.

For buffet, serves 12.

Green Tomatoes Stuffed with Meat (Domates Verdes Inchidos con Karne)

Stuffed with lean beef and baked in a sauce of their own pulp and celery, green tomatoes attain an unusual taste, with the celery emphasizing the tartness of the green tomato. Celery and tomato join in harmonious mixture in this dish.

12 large, round, unripe, green tomatoes
1½ pounds chopped lean beef
1 slice day-old bread, soaked in water and squeezed dry
1 egg, lightly beaten
1 teaspoon salt
½ teaspoon ground pepper
2 tablespoons chopped parsley
2 tablespoons water

4 tablespoons light vegetable oil
flour for dipping
5 stalks celery with their leaves, chopped coarsely
2 tablespoons flour dissolved in 2 tablespoons water
salt
pepper
1 tablespoon sugar

Wash and cut off one-quarter from the top of each tomato. Remove the inedible crown from the top quarter and chop the rest. Scoop out the tomatoes, chop the insides, and reserve together with the chopped top for the sauce.

In a large mixing bowl, mix the beef with the soaked bread, egg, salt, ground pepper and parsley. Add 2 tablespoons water to the mixture and blend in. Stuff the tomatoes firmly.

In a heavy skillet, heat 2 tablespoons of the oil. Spread the flour on a flat surface. Take each tomato in the palm of your hand, turn it upside down and dip the top gently in the flour. Fry upside down in the hot oil for a minute or two, to seal in the stuffing. Turn the tomatoes and fry for another few minutes. Remove with a slotted spoon and reserve.

Wipe skillet clean and heat the remaining oil. Saute together the chopped stalks of celery and tomato pulp for several minutes. Add the 2 tablespoons flour blended with the water to the pan. Let it thicken, stirring all the while. Add salt to taste, ground pepper and the sugar.

In a deep, wide baking dish, large enough to hold all the tomatoes standing upright on one level, pour half the celery-tomato mixture. Spread across the bottom, and arrange the tomatoes on top. Spoon the remaining mixture over the tomatoes, cover with aluminum foil, and bake in a 350° oven for ½ hour. Uncover, and bake for another 30 minutes. If, when you uncover the casserole, the pan seems too dry, add ¾ cup bouillon to the pan.

Serves 12.

Stuffed Red Peppers
(Gambas Inchidos con Karne)

The peppers we used for this dish (bonnet peppers) were perfectly round, plump, sweet and a deep Chinese red. But the same filling serves green and sweet yellow and red peppers as well, and each type of pepper provides its own distinctive taste. Try a platter of different peppers of varying colors.

12 sweet red peppers	ground pepper
1 pound ground lean beef	2 tablespoons water
¼ cup rice	2 tablespoons light vegetable oil
1 onion, chopped finely	1 cup tomato puree
1 tomato, peeled, seeded and chopped	1 cup water
	juice of ½ lemon
2 tablespoons chopped parsley	pinch of sugar
1 teaspoon salt	2 stalks celery, whole with leaves

Remove the crowns and seeds from the peppers, wash and drain upside down.

In a bowl, mix the meat, raw rice, chopped onion, chopped tomato, chopped parsley, salt, pepper, and 2 tablespoons water. Blend well. Fill the peppers three-quarters full, leaving room for the rice to swell.

In a flameproof baking dish large enough to hold the peppers upright on one level, heat the oil, add the tomato puree, add the cup of water, lemon juice, sugar and celery and cook the sauce for 10 minutes. Taste and add salt and pepper.

Stand the peppers carefully in the sauce, lower the heat, cover with foil, and cook for 20 minutes. Remove the foil and bake the peppers for another 45 minutes in a 350° oven.

For buffet, serves 12.

Stuffed Zucchini in Fresh Tomato Sauce (Kalavasikas Inchidos con Karne in Sos di Domates Frescos)

We stuffed and baked our zucchini upright. It takes a bit of practice to scoop out just the right amount of flesh to leave a firm, intact, but not too bulky casing. But if you begin with large enough zucchini and scrape carefully with a vegetable peeler or even a small teaspoon, it shouldn't be too difficult.

2 pounds medium-sized zucchini	9 tablespoons chopped dill
3 tablespoons light vegetable oil	4 tablespoons chopped parsley
1 medium onion, chopped finely	salt
¼ cup rice	pepper
2 pounds ground lean beef	¾ cup water
8 large ripe tomatoes, peeled, seeded and chopped	juice of ½ lemon
1 teaspoon salt	1 tablespoon sugar
½ teaspoon pepper	2 stalks celery, whole with their leaves

Wash the zucchini, cut them in half widthwise and prepare them for stuffing by gently digging out the center pulp with an apple corer or potato peeler, leaving a quarter-inch edge to the hole. Discard the pulp. Snip off the end of each in order that they will stand upright in the baking dish. In a heavy skillet, heat half the oil and saute the onion lightly. Add the rice and cook until it is transparent. Remove from heat. Add the meat, 2 tablespoons of the chopped tomatoes, 1 teaspoon salt, ½ teaspoon pepper, half the dill and half the parsley. Mix well.

Stuff the zucchini ¾ full, leaving place for the rice to swell. Stand upright on a plate and set aside.

In a flameproof baking dish large enough to hold the zucchini upright, heat the remaining oil and add the remaining tomatoes, ¾ cup water, salt to taste, more ground pepper, the remaining chopped parsley and dill, the lemon juice, sugar and celery stalks and cook over a medium fire for 10 minutes. Taste, correct seasoning and lower the heat.

Arrange the stuffed zucchini upright, cover with foil, and cook for 30 minutes. Uncover and finish cooking in a 350° oven for another 30 minutes.

Serves 6.

Stuffed Zucchini
(Kalavasikas Inchidos con Karne)

Garlicked, carmelized zucchini. The zucchini is stuffed with nicely seasoned beef and the pulp is reserved for the sauce. When you core the zucchini take care not to cut too deep or you may dig a hole through the ends.

2 pounds medium-sized zucchini	2 tablespoons water
1 pound lean ground beef	2 tablespoons light vegetable oil
½ cup fresh bread crumbs	6 garlic cloves, peeled and whole
½ teaspoon salt	3 tablespoons sugar
ground pepper	2 tablespoons water
2 tablespoons chopped dill	salt
1 egg, lightly beaten	pepper

Wash, scrape and chop the zucchini in half across the middle (not lengthwise). With an apple corer or the end of a potato peeler, gently dig out the center pulp, leaving a quarter-inch width. Chop the pulp and reserve for the sauce. Slice the tiniest tip off each bottom, just enough that the zucchini will stand upright in the baking dish. Turn upside down and allow to rest.

In a mixing bowl, put the beef, bread crumbs, salt, pepper, chopped dill and the egg. Add 2 tablespoons water and blend well. Stuff the zucchini full with the mixture.

In a flameproof baking dish large enough to hold the zucchini upright, heat the oil and saute the whole garlic cloves until they are a deep brown color. Discard quickly before they burn. Add the sugar and cook until it becomes golden. Add 2 tablespoons water and the pulp of the zucchini. Salt to taste, add a grinding of pepper and cook for two or three minutes.

Arrange the stuffed zucchini upright on the bed of garlic-flavored zucchini pulp, cover with aluminum foil and cook over a low heat for 30 minutes. Uncover and finish cooking in a 350° oven for another 30 minutes.

Serves 6.

Meatballs with Zucchini
(Albondigas con Kalavasikas)

This easy to prepare dish makes a delicious light meal when accompanied by rice.

2 pounds medium-sized zucchini	½ cup water
coarse salt	1 pound lean ground beef or veal
3 tablespoons light vegetable oil	2 tablespoons flour dissolved in 2
4 cloves garlic (2 whole, 2	tablespoons water
crushed)	½ teaspoon ground pepper
2 tablespoons sugar	2 tablespoons chopped dill
2 teaspoons salt	

Wash and cube the zucchini without peeling. Sprinkle with coarse salt and drain for ½ hour. Wash away the salt and pat the zucchini dry.

In a heavy skillet with cover, heat the oil, saute 2 of the garlic cloves, whole, until brown. Discard the garlic. Add the sugar, let it just turn brown, then add the cubed zucchini. Mix well and cook over a low heat for 10 minutes. Add 1 teaspoon salt and ½ cup water.

Place the meat in a mixing bowl. Add the flour and water mixture and mix well into the meat. Add the second teaspoon of salt, ground pepper and the chopped dill. Mix again. Shape into small one-inch balls and gently add the meatballs to the zucchini in the skillet. Cover and cook for ½ hour over a low heat. Uncover, add a dash of pepper and the remaining garlic, crushed. Finish cooking uncovered in a 350° oven for another 30 minutes.

Serves 6.

Stuffed Eggplant
(Merendjen a Inchidos con Karne)

Who doesn't enjoy stuffed eggplant? A medium-sized eggplant makes an ample, attractive casing for this beef filling. Serve one-half if serving as an appetizer, two halves for a main course, or all together on a buffet platter alternating with stuffed red and green peppers or zucchini.

6 medium-sized eggplants	1 egg, lightly beaten
coarse salt	¾ cup water
1 pound ground lean beef	pinch of sugar
1 teaspoon salt	salt
½ teaspoon pepper	pepper
3 tablespoons chopped parsley	3 tablespoons olive oil
4 tablespoons tomato paste	

Halve the eggplants lengthwise without peeling. Scoop out the center of each half, leaving a shell of one inch width. Discard the pulp. Sprinkle the shell with coarse salt, turn over and drain for ½ hour. Wash away the salt and dry the inside with a paper towel.

In a bowl, mix the meat, breadcrumbs, 1 teaspoon salt, ½ teaspoon pepper, chopped parsley, and 1 tablespoon of the tomato paste. Bind with the beaten egg and stuff the eggplants with this mixture. In a small saucepan, dilute the remaining tomato paste in ¾ cup water. Add the sugar, more ground pepper and salt, and the olive oil. Cook for a few minutes.

Oil a baking dish and arrange the eggplant halves in a single layer, pour over the sauce, cover with foil, and bake in a 350° oven for an hour. Remove the foil and bake for another ¾ hour.

Serves 12.

Braised Meatballs with Eggplant (Albondigas con Merendjena)

One of the most popular Sephardic dishes. The eggplant pulp prepared with plenty of garlic and a dash of sugar makes a novel background for the meatballs. Preparation isn't difficult, but it depends on the grilling or roasting of the whole eggplant. The trick: make sure that the entire skin turns evenly black. You may have to move the eggplant around a bit to achieve this, but brown spots indicate that the flesh underneath is under-cooked. Also, be sure to drain the eggplant thoroughly of all its bitter juices.

3 eggplants	1 pound ground lean beef
4 tablespoons light vegetable oil	2 tablespoons flour dissolved in 2
6 cloves garlic, crushed	tablespoons water
1 teaspoon salt	3 tablespoons chopped parsley
¼ teaspoon sugar	½ teaspoon ground pepper

Grill the eggplants over an open fire, if available, or under the broiler on all sides until they are blackened outside and soft inside. Remove them to a colander and allow to rest until cool. When they are cool, peel off the blackened outer skin, chop the pulps coarsely and replace in the colander to allow them to drain off their bitter juices.

In a heavy lidded skillet, heat the oil and saute one tablespoon of the crushed garlic. When it begins to sizzle, add the drained chopped eggplant pulp. Lower the heat and cook for 15 minutes, stirring often to prevent sticking. Add ½ teaspoon salt and the sugar.

While the eggplant is cooking, put the beef into a small mixing bowl and knead the flour-water mixture into it. Add ½ teaspoon salt, the parsley and pepper. Mix well and shape into small 1-inch balls. As you shape the balls, drop each one into the eggplant. When all the meatballs are in, cover the skillet and cook slowly for another 30 minutes, checking every now and again to make sure the eggplant is not sticking. If it begins to stick, add ¼ cup of water to the skillet. At the end of 30 minutes, uncover, add the remaining garlic and more salt if necessary and place in a 350° oven for another 20–30 minutes, until a crust is formed.

Serves 6.

Meat-Stuffed Vine Leaves
(Yaprakitos)

The sauce, a conglomeration of sweet honey, fresh-tasting dill, tangy lemon and tomato puree, gives this traditional Greek dish its specifically Sephardic flavor. If you can get the fresh young, light-green grape leaves, these are of course the tenderest. Should you find only the older leaves, cut out the tough central rib. And as for the canned vine leaves, be sure to rinse them well. The raw rice in this recipe, as in others, swells in cooking, but the heavy plate on top will keep the packages from bursting.

30–40 grape leaves, either young fresh ones or tinned	**The Sauce:**
	1 cup water
1 pound ground lean beef	¼ cup tomato paste
2 tablespoons water	1 tablespoon honey
¼ cup rice	1 teaspoon salt
1 medium-sized yellow onion, grated	½ teaspoon pepper
	juice of ½ lemon
1 teaspoon salt	2 tablespoons chopped dill
½ teaspoon pepper	
1 tablespoon chopped dill	

If you are using the tinned variety of vine leaves, wash them well before using. Fresh leaves should be blanched for a minute in boiling water.

For the filling, mix well in a bowl the chopped beef, 2 tablespoons water, the uncooked rice, grated onion, salt, pepper and 1 tablespoon of the dill. Place a vine leaf flat and put a dessertspoon of the filling into the center of the leaf. Make a small parcel by folding up the stem end first and then the sides. Roll up the leaf and squeeze as tightly as possible. Repeat until all the leaves and filling have been used. Pack the rolls into a casserole dish in layers.

Make a sauce of one cup water, the tomato paste, honey, salt, pepper, the juice of half a lemon and the remaining chopped dill. Pour the sauce over the leaves. Press a plate well down on the *yaprakitos* to hold them firm and cook gently for an hour over low heat.

Serves 8.

Stuffed Chard Leaves
(Yaprakes di Pazi)

Chard is perhaps an unusual wrapping, but it's extremely delicate in taste. Don't throw out the white stalks. They are very good eaten as an appetizer or side dish (see p. 17).

(see p. 17)

2 pounds Swiss chard, or kale	2 tablespoons chopped parsley
4 tablespoons light vegetable oil	¾ cup water
1 yellow onion, finely chopped	juice of ½ lemon
¼ cup rice, washed	salt
1 pound ground veal or lean beef	ground pepper
1 teaspoon salt	¼ teaspoon sugar
½ teaspoon pepper	lemon quarters

Wash the chard leaves well, remove the white center stalk and cut the larger leaves in half vertically. Pour boiling water over the leaves, rinse them with cold water and leave to drain in a colander.

In a skillet heat 2½ tablespoons of the oil, saute the chopped onion until transparent, add the rice and cook until it turns pearly. Remove from heat, add the meat, salt, ground pepper, 1 tablespoon of the chopped parsley and ¼ cup of the water.

To fill, lay out a single leaf of chard, put a teaspoon of the mixture in the center and make a little parcel by rolling as tightly as possible. Squeeze gently. Pack the little rolls into a pan layer on layer. Mix together ½ cup of water, the remaining 1½ tablespoon oil, the lemon juice, more salt, grind of pepper, sugar and the remaining chopped parsley.

Press a plate well down to keep the rolls in place. Cover and cook for ¾ hour on a low heat. Uncover and correct seasoning in the sauce before serving with lemon quarters on the side.

Serves 6–8.

Stuffed Cabbage Leaves
(Yaprakes di Kol Dulce)

There probably isn't a country in Europe or the Middle East that doesn't have its version of stuffed cabbage. Ours is small and tart, and well worth making in large quantities since the taste improves with reheating. Serve with boiled potatoes for a hearty winter meal.

1 firm white cabbage, whole	2 tablespoons water
3 tablespoons light vegetable oil	1 teaspoon salt
1 onion, chopped finely	½ teaspoon ground pepper
¼ cup rice	1 cup water
1 pound lean beef, ground	½ teaspoon sugar
½ cup tomato paste	juice of 1½ lemons

Remove the hard part of the cabbage stem. Blanch the whole cabbage in salted boiling water for 5 minutes and drain in a colander.

In a skillet, saute the chopped onion in 1 tablespoon of the oil until transparent, add the rice and cook until it turns pearly. Remove from heat. Mix in the meat, 2 tablespoons of the tomato paste, 2 tablespoons water, salt and ground pepper.

Gently separate the cabbage leaves and cut each leaf off from the hard stem. Put a heaped spoon of the filling into the center of each leaf and make a parcel by folding the stem end over first, then the sides. Roll them up as tightly as possible. Arrange the stuffed leaves closely together in a large saucepan.

Mix together the remaining tomato paste, water, salt, ground pepper, sugar, remaining 2 tablespoons of oil and the lemon juice. Pour over the leaves. Press a plate well down on the *yaprakes* to keep them in place. Cover and cook over low heat for 1½ hours. Serve hot.

Serves 6–8.

Stuffed Pickled Cabbage Leaves
(Yaprakes di Kol Agra)

We always had our pickled cabbage heads stored for the winter in barrels, and stuffed pickled cabbage was a staple winter dish. If you have a Balkan specialty shop nearby that sells the whole cabbage pickled, this is a dish worth trying. A recipe for pickled cabbage quarters is on p. 188.

1 pickled white cabbage, whole, or 4 quarters	2 tablespoons water
	1 teaspoon salt
2 tablespoons oil	½ teaspoon pepper
1 yellow onion, chopped finely	½ cup tomato paste
¼ cup rice	1 cup water
1 pound ground lean beef	1 tablespoon sugar

Remove the leaves of the cabbage and wash well in water. Drain in a colander.

In a skillet heat the oil and gently saute the onion until transparent. Add the rice and continue to cook until the rice turns pearly. Remove from heat and add the ground beef, 2 tablespoons water, the salt, pepper and 2 tablespoons of the tomato paste. Mix well.

Gently separate the cabbage leaves, and cut off each leaf from the center core. Place a large spoonful of the stuffing on each leaf, roll up tightly and arrange the stuffed leaves side by side in a large saucepan. Mix together the remaining tomato paste, the cup of water and the sugar and pour over the leaves. Cover the saucepan and cook over low heat for 1 hour. Uncover, and bake in a 350° oven for another hour. Serve hot.

Serves 6–8.

Stuffed Artichokes
(Articho Ienos con Karne)

Artichokes must be one of the world's most luxurious vegetables, and meat-stuffed artichokes one of the most impressive dishes at a small dinner or luncheon party. With just a bit of practice and patience, you'll soon become adept at the slightly intricate preparation, which will be easier if you use a very sharp knife.

12 globe artichokes	1 yellow onion, chopped finely
½ lemon	2 tablespoons breadcrumbs
large bowl of cold water	1 teaspoon salt
2 tablespoons flour	½ teaspoon pepper
2 teaspoons coarse salt	3 tablespoons chopped dill
juice of 2 lemons	¼ cup light vegetable oil
1 pound ground lean beef	

Remove the tough outer leaves and cut off the upper half of each artichoke. Slice each bottom flat so the artichokes can stand comfortably upright. With a paring knife and dessert spoon scoop out the hairy choke and rub all the cut parts with a lemon half. Immerse the treated artichokes in a bowl of water into which has been mixed the flour, coarse salt and the juice of one lemon.

In another bowl mix the meat, chopped onion, breadcrumbs, salt, pepper and 1 tablespoon of the dill. Stuff the center hole of each artichoke from where the choke has been removed and arrange in a baking dish.

Mix the juice of the remaining lemon, the remaining 2 tablespoons of chopped dill and the oil and pour over the artichokes. Cover with foil and bake in a 375° oven for one hour.

Serves 12.

Fried Stuffed Artichokes
(Articho Ienos Fritos)

Similar to the previous dish. But here the stuffed artichoke is first coated in egg and flour and fried, then baked in a thick bouillon broth for a heartier and more substantial result.

12 globe artichokes	1 teaspoon salt
½ lemon	½ teaspoon pepper
juice of 1 lemon	2 tablespoons chopped dill
large bowl of cold water	1 tablespoon light vegetable oil
2 tablespoons flour	1 tablespoon water
2 teaspoons coarse salt	2 eggs, lightly beaten
1 pound ground lean beef	flour for coating
1 yellow onion, grated	oil for frying
2 tablespoons breadcrumbs	¾ cup strong hot beef stock

Remove the tough outer leaves and slice off the upper half of the artichoke. Remove the stem, cut the bottoms flat with a paring knife. With a dessert spoon, remove the hairy center of each artichoke. Wipe the cut parts with ½ lemon and plunge the artichokes into a bowl filled with water mixed with 2 tablespoons flour, 2 teaspoons coarse salt and the juice of 1 lemon.

In another bowl, mix the meat, grated onion, breadcrumbs, salt, pepper and chopped dill. Add the oil and water and blend well. Stuff the artichokes with the meat mixture.

Heat a good ½ inch of frying oil in a heavy skillet. Dip the stuffed artichokes into the beaten egg and coat well with flour. Fry until well browned on all sides. Remove with slotted spoon and arrange side by side in a shallow baking pan. Pour stock around the artichokes. Bake in a 350° oven for ¾ hour.

Serves 12.

Moussaka
(Moussaka)

There's always much to praise in the full-bodied flavor of a good eggplant moussaka. The tomato paste diluted in bouillon keeps the dish moist, while the fresh tomatoes in the middle add a delightful fillip.

3 medium-sized eggplants
coarse salt
frying oil
1 large yellow onion, chopped finely
1½ pounds chopped lean beef
pulp of an additional small eggplant, baked whole until soft and pulp scooped out
¼ cup fresh breadcrumbs
2 tablespoons chopped parsley

1 teaspoon salt
½ teaspoon pepper
6 garlic cloves, crushed
2 large eggs, lightly beaten
salt
1 teaspoon sugar
2 large tomatoes, sliced
3 tablespoons tomato paste
2 bouillon cubes, dissolved in ½ cup boiling water

Wash and slice the eggplant into ½-inch slices without peeling. Sprinkle with coarse salt and let stand in a colander for ½–1 hour. Wash away salt and pat dry.

In a heavy skillet, heat 2 tablespoons of oil and fry the eggplant on both sides until golden. Drain the slices on a paper towel.

Wipe the skillet clean and saute the chopped onion in another 2 tablespoons oil. Add the meat and cook until it turns color. Remove from heat, mix in the pulp of the small baked eggplant, the breadcrumbs, chopped parsley, salt, pepper and a teaspoon of the crushed garlic. Add the lightly beaten eggs and mix well.

Line the bottom of an oiled baking dish with half the eggplant slices, sprinkle some salt, sugar and part of the remaining squeezed garlic over, and spread the entire meat mixture across the slices. Spread the sliced tomatoes on top. Cover with the remaining eggplant slices, overlapping them to completely cover. Sprinkle with more salt and sugar and the remaining garlic.

In a small bowl, dissolve the tomato paste in the bouillon and pour evenly over the moussaka. Bake in a 350° oven for 1½ hours.

Serves 6–8.

Zucchini Moussaka
(Moussaka di Kalavasika)

Voila! The standard eggplant moussaka transformed into a delicate zucchini casserole. Wonderful in mid-summer when zucchini is plentiful and tender, and when the palate craves light and lifting foods.

3 pounds medium-sized zucchini	½ teaspoon pepper
coarse salt	4 cloves garlic, crushed
flour to dip	3 tablespoons chopped parsley
frying oil	2 eggs, slightly beaten
1 large yellow onion, chopped	2 tablespoons tomato paste
finely	1–2 bouillon cubes dissolved in ½
1 pound chopped lean veal	cup boiling water
1 teaspoon salt	½ teaspoon sugar

Wash and slice the zucchini lengthwise into ¼ inch strips. Sprinkle with coarse salt, and allow to drain in a colander for ½ hour. Wash away the salt and dry well.

Dip the zucchini slices in flour and fry in hot oil on both sides until golden brown. Arrange on paper towels to drain off the excessive oil. In a clean skillet, heat 2 tablespoons oil and saute the chopped onion until transparent. Add the meat and cook until it whitens. Remove from heat, add salt, ground pepper, 2 of the crushed garlic cloves and chopped parsley. Add beaten eggs and mix well.

Line the bottom of an oiled baking dish with half of the fried zucchini slices. Sprinkle salt, sugar and a bit of the remaining crushed garlic over it.

Spread the meat mixture over the zucchini and cover with another layer of zucchini.

In a small bowl, dissolve the tomato paste in the hot bouillon, add a pinch of salt, the sugar, a grinding of pepper and the remaining crushed garlic. Pour over the zucchini and bake in a 300° oven for 1 hour.

Serves 6–8.

Potato Moussaka
(Moussaka di Kartofis)

Meat and potatoes may sound dull, but this moussaka is proof to the contrary. A filling winter dish, it is both easy to prepare and guaranteed to please. The overlapping potatoes absorb the sealed-in juices of the beef. Be sure that the crust is nice and golden before you remove from the oven.

2 pounds potatoes, peeled and sliced into ¼ inch width
3 tablespoons light vegetable oil
1 large yellow onion, chopped finely
1 pound ground lean beef
1 teaspoon salt
½ teaspoon pepper
3 tablespoons chopped dill

1 large ripe tomato, peeled, seeded and chopped
3 eggs
2 bouillon cubes dissolved in 1 cup boiling water
2 tablespoons tomato paste
ground pepper
½ teaspoon sugar

Slice the potatoes and set aside.

In a skillet heat the oil and saute the onions until transparent. Add the meat and continue cooking until it turns color. Remove from heat, add salt, pepper, half of the chopped dill, and the chopped tomato. Mix well and blend one beaten egg into the mixture.

In a well-oiled, deep baking dish arrange half the sliced potatoes. The slices should slightly overlap one another. Spread the entire meat mixture and cover with the remaining potato slices, again overlapping. Dissolve the tomato paste into the cup of bouillon, add pepper, sugar and the remaining chopped dill. Beat the two remaining eggs and add to the liquid. Pour the sauce over the moussaka and bake in a 350° oven for one hour or until the potatoes are done and the moussaka has a light brown crust.

Serves 6–8.

Spinach and Meat Rissoles
(Fritas di Spinaka)

I have always found spinach one of the most delectable of greens. Joined with beef in a breaded and crisply fried patty and garnished with lemon wedges, we ate it at home as a sprightly complement to chicken or roast.

2 pounds spinach	¼ teaspoon ground nutmeg
1 pound ground lean beef	3 eggs, lightly beaten
¼ cup fresh breadcrumbs	flour for dusting
1 teaspoon salt	oil for deep frying
½ teaspoon pepper	lemon wedges

Wash the spinach well and put into a large pan without draining. Cook over a high heat only until the spinach wilts (2 or 3 minutes). Remove to colander and when cool enough to handle, squeeze out as much moisture as possible. Chop finely.

In a separate bowl, mix the meat, breadcrumbs, salt, ground pepper and nutmeg. Knead the spinach into the mixture and add the eggs. Shape into small patties, roll in flour and fry in hot oil until brown and crisp. Serve with wedges of lemons.

Makes about 20 rissoles.

Potato and Beef Rissoles
(Fritas di Kartof)

If there is such a thing as a fail-proof dish, it is this sturdy potato-beef patty, appealing to both children and adults. Acutally, Mother often served vegetables patties as a side dish to a chicken or roast. And though the kind naturally varied with the season, this, like the potato it's made from, was in year-round demand.

1 pound potatoes, peeled and quartered	½ teaspoon pepper
½ pound ground lean beef	½ teaspoon ground nutmeg
3 eggs, lightly beaten	2 tablespoons chopped parsley
1 teaspoon salt	5–6 tablespoons flour
	oil for frying

Boil the potatoes in salted water until soft. Drain and return the potatoes to the dry pan. Shake the pan over the heat to remove excess moisture from the potatoes. Remove them and mash.

In a separate bowl mix the meat, eggs, salt, ground pepper, nutmeg and chopped parsley. Add the mashed potatoes and mix well. Shape into small patties, roll in flour and fry in hot oil. Drain on paper towels.

Makes about 20 rissoles.

Leek and Beef Rissoles
(Fritas di Prasa)

Back home, the deserving leek was very much appreciated, and these leek and beef patties were one of our favorite standbys with chicken or roast veal. We enjoyed them all winter through early spring, especially during Passover, which wasn't allowed to go by without them, in plenty.

2 pounds leeks	½ teaspoon ground pepper
1 large yellow onion, whole	3 eggs
1 small celery root (celeriac), peeled and whole	oil for frying
	juice of ½ lemon
1 pound ground lean beef or veal	lemon wedges
1 teaspoon salt	

Slice off only the toughest green ends of the leeks. Wash well and slice them into 2 inch lengths. Parboil together with the onion for 10 minutes. Add the small celery head and continue cooking until the vegetables are soft. Drain well in a colander and chop finely or blend in a food processor.

In a separate bowl mix the ground meat, salt, ground pepper and 2 lightly beaten eggs. Add the leek mixture and knead well. Shape into small patties, dip them into a well-beaten egg, fry in hot oil until golden and crisp. Before serving, squeeze some lemon juice on top. Serve with lemon wedges.

Makes about 25–30 patties.

VEGETABLE SIDE DISHES

Vegetable Side Dishes

In the olden days when seasons were seasons and the distinction between them unblurred by the presence in the markets of vegetables coming from warmer climates and greenhouses — to say nothing of frozen and canned foods — every cook knew just what dishes she could or couldn't make when. Yet there was certainly no shortage. With leafy greens in the spring and summer, root vegetables in the winter, and beans and cabbage the year round, there was — and still is — plenty to inspire the imaginative cook.

You can readily see — and taste — for yourself the countless themes to be played on. The vegetables can be cooked separately or in combination. They can be simply boiled and seasoned, deep or shallow fried, stuffed with rice or other vegetables, or lightly sauteed and then stewed in a delicate, exotic or robust sauce.

Our vegetable side dishes differ from the first course vegetables which are usually served chilled. Yet, like the first course dishes, they are often filling enough to be a course in themselves.

Garlic-Flavored Zucchini
(Kalavasikas con Ajo)

Burnt sugar and garlic, this uniquely Sephardic couple, give an entirely new dimension to the familiar zucchini. As the dish has an assertive flavor, it is a lifting accompaniment to roast veal and other delicate meats.

2½ pounds baby zucchini	¼ cup water
3 tablespoons olive oil	½ teaspoon salt
6 cloves of garlic, peeled and halved	freshly ground pepper
2 tablespoons sugar	

Wash and cube the zucchini.

In a lidded saucepan, saute the 6 garlic cloves uncovered in the olive oil until they are well browned. (Don't let them burn.) Discard the garlic. Add the sugar to the pan and carefully cook until the sugar just turns brown. Add the cubed zucchini and mix gently, to coat the zucchini with the sugar. Add ¼ cup of water and the salt, and cover. Cook over a low heat for 30 minutes. Uncover and cook briskly until all the liquid has evaporated. Add a good grinding of fresh pepper and serve hot. Serve with any light meat or poultry.

Serves 6–8.

Zucchini with Tomatoes and Onions (Kalavasikas con Domates e Sivoya)

Zucchini, tomatoes, and onions — this typically Mediterranean melange — are lightly sauteed, generously seasoned with garlic, pepper and dill, and briefly baked. The result is a zestful, colorful dish that goes well with any meat.

2 pounds baby zucchini	3 cloves garlic, crushed
3 tablespoons olive oil	½ teaspoon salt
1 large onion, thinly sliced	ground pepper
3 ripe tomatoes, peeled, seeded and quartered	2 tablespoons chopped fresh dill

Wash and slice the zucchini lengthwise into ¼-inch slices.

In a heavy skillet heat 2 tablespoons of the olive oil and saute the sliced onion until soft. Remove with a slotted spoon, and arrange in the bottom of a shallow baking dish. In the same heavy skillet, in the same oil, saute the zucchini and spread them over the onions. Again, in the same skillet saute the quartered tomatoes lightly. Arrange around and over the zucchini. Add the remaining oil to the skillet and squeeze in the garlic. Remove from heat, add salt, plenty of freshly ground pepper and dill, and spoon with all the pan juices over the vegetables in the baking dish. Bake in a 375° oven for 20–25 minutes.

Serves 6.

Stewed Zucchini, Eggplant and Potatoes
(Kalavasikas con Mirindjenas i Kartofes)

To the ubiquitous eggplant-zucchini combination, my mother added potatoes, which turned this side dish into a delicious meal in itself. Served with a cooling bowl of yoghurt and crunchy fresh bread, it makes a delightful summer lunch.

3 tablespoons olive oil
1 large onion, chopped coarsely
2 small eggplants, unpeeled, cubed
1 pound zucchini, unpeeled, cubed
2 red peppers, seeded and cubed
3 ripe tomatoes, peeled, seeded and chopped coarsely
2 large potatoes, peeled and cubed
1 teaspoon salt
½ teaspoon sugar
freshly ground pepper
2 tablespoons chopped fresh dill
juice of ½ lemon

In a large, heavy, shallow, flameproof casserole, heat one tablespoon of the oil and saute the onion until soft. Remove with slotted spoon and set aside in a large bowl. Saute the eggplant and zucchini for 5 minutes each in the same way and add to the onions in the bowl. Do the same with the peppers, remove and set aside with the other vegetables. Add the tomatoes to the casserole, saute for a minute or two and return the other vegetables to the pan. Add the cubed potatoes, the remaining olive oil, the salt, sugar, a good grinding of pepper, the chopped dill and lemon juice. Cover and cook over a low heat for 15 minutes. Uncover, add water if it seems too dry, and cook for another 15 minutes.

Serves 6.

Zucchini Fritters
(with Yoghurt Sauce)
(Fritas di Kalavisikas)

The hotter the oil, the crisper the zucchini will be. Dunked in a smooth, well-seasoned yoghurt sauce, these dainty morsels make a wonderful summer entree.

2½ pounds baby zucchini
flour for coating
oil for frying

The Sauce:
3 cups yoghurt
1 tablespoon vinegar

3 tablespoons olive oil
3 cloves garlic, crushed
½ teaspoon salt
¼ teaspoon sugar
1 generous handful of chopped dill
or fresh mint

Wash and slice marrows lengthwise about ¼ inch thick. Dip in flour and deep-fry in hot oil until golden.

Drain on paper towels and serve with yoghurt sauce.

Yoghurt Sauce: Whisk together in a bowl the yoghurt, vinegar, oil, crushed garlic, salt and sugar. Add the fresh chopped dill or mint. Serve heaped into a bowl accompanying the zucchini platter.

Another way of making these fritters is to dip the sliced zucchini into a batter before deep frying. Drain and serve in the same way.

Serves 6–8.

Cubed Eggplant
(Kvartikus di Mirindjenas)

One always associates eggplant with the Mediterranean. Well, it actually originated in the Indies and was brought to Europe only in the 19th century — to become one of our most resourceful vegetables. This particular version makes a gratifying accompaniment to a succulent beef roast.

2 medium-sized eggplants, unpeeled, cubed	pinch of sugar
	¼ cup water
3 tablespoons olive oil	4–5 cloves of garlic, crushed
1 large onion, coarsely chopped	2 tablespoons chopped fresh dill
salt	ground black pepper

Sprinkle the cubed eggplant with coarse salt, and let drain in a colander for at least half an hour. Wash off the salt, squeeze the eggplants of excess water, and dry in a clean cloth.

In a heavy skillet (with a lid) heat the olive oil and saute the onion uncovered, until soft. Add the eggplant and continue to saute for 2–3 minutes. Add salt, sugar, ¼ cup water, cover and cook for 10 minutes. Uncover.

Add the crushed garlic, chopped dill and a grinding of black pepper. Taste, correct seasoning, and serve.

Serves 6.

Stewed Eggplant
(Mirindjenas Gizada)

Eggplant has a remarkable capacity for absorbing the flavors it's cooked in without losing its own. In this recipe, generous quantities of garlic and dill enliven the eggplant's deep, full-bodied richness, while the green peppers and tomatoes provide a painterly contrast of colors and textures. Served hot or at room temperature, it makes a smashing buffet dish.

3 medium eggplants, unpeeled, sliced widthwise in ½ inch slices	3 tomatoes, sliced
3 tablespoons olive oil	3 peppers, red or green, seeded and sliced into rings
2 onions, sliced in rings	3–4 garlic cloves, crushed
1 teaspoon salt	fresh pepper
¼ teaspoon sugar	1 handful of chopped dill

Sprinkle the eggplant slices with coarse salt and let drain for ½ hour. Wash away the salt and drain again.

In a shallow casserole with a lid, put 1½ tablespoons of the oil, spread a layer of half the onion slices, cover with half the eggplant slices, sprinkle salt and a large pinch of sugar over the eggplant, add half the tomatoes and half the peppers, and some crushed garlic. Repeat procedure with the remaining vegetables. Add more salt, sugar, crushed garlic, a good grinding of pepper and dill on top. Pour the remaining 2 tablespoons of olive oil over the top, cover and cook over a low heat. After 10–15 minutes, uncover, add a little water if it seems dry, and finish cooking uncovered for another 20 minutes.

Serves 8.

Melange of Eggplant and Zucchini
(Comida di Mirindjena con Kalavasa)

Every Mediterranean country has its bright, tasty melange of peppers, zucchini, onions and eggplant. Ours, of course, was distinguished by the aromatic pungency of fresh chopped dill added at the very last minute. This dish is an easy success. All you have to do is make sure to thoroughly desalt and drain the eggplant and zucchini and then cook each of the vegetables in its due order and time.

2 medium eggplants, unpeeled, cubed	4 tomatoes, peeled, seeded and chopped coarsely
4 medium zucchini, cubed	½ teaspoon table salt
coarse salt	pinch of sugar
3 tablespoons light vegetable oil	¼ cup water
1 large onion, sliced	2 tablespoons chopped dill
2 green peppers, seeded and sliced into rings	freshly ground pepper

Mix and salt generously the eggplant and zucchini cubes and drain for at least half an hour in a colander. Wash off the salt and drain again. In a heavy skillet with a lid, heat the oil and saute the onion slices, uncovered, lightly. Add the sliced peppers and cook together for another few minutes. Add the tomatoes, cover and cook for ten minutes. Uncover, add the eggplant and zucchini cubes, the salt, sugar and ½ cup water. Cover and cook again for 15–20 minutes. Uncover, add the chopped dill and plenty of ground pepper. Taste for seasoning and serve.

Serves 8.

Stewed Eggplant Fritters
(Fritas di Mirindjenas)

The: eggplant slices, individually fried and then simmered in bouillon, were a Friday evening staple. Though it meant a lot of work, an enormous quantity invariably found its way to our table. The dish can be varied by dipping the slices in batter before frying, or in a slightly beaten egg to which you've added a teaspoon of water and a pinch of salt.

3 large eggplants, unpeeled, sliced widthwise into ½-inch thick slices	salt
	pinch of sugar
coarse salt	pepper
flour	3 cups beef stock
oil for frying	

Sprinkle the eggplant slices with coarse salt and drain for half an hour. Wash away the salt and drain again.

Heat enough oil to cover bottom of a large skillet (with a lid). Pat dry the eggplant slices, dust with flour and fry the slices a few at a time until lightly browned. Leave to drain on paper towels.

When all the eggplant slices have been fried, wipe out any excess oil from the skillet and replace the fried slices side by side in layers, sprinkling each layer with salt, a pinch of sugar and freshly ground pepper.

Boil the beef stock and pour over the fritters. Cover the skillet and simmer over low heat until all the liquid is absorbed.

Serves 8.

Stuffed Baby Eggplants
(Ymam Bayalda)

This recipe, we were told, came directly from the court of the Turkish Imam. The tiny baby eggplants — a small, greyish variety available in Greek and other Mediterranean vegetable stores — were stuffed with a sweetish mixture of onions, raisins and parsley, individually topped with a whole clove of garlic, lightly sauteed and baked in plenty of olive oil to produce one of the most dainty delicacies to intrigue your palate. With only a fresh salad, it makes a rare and unexpected luncheon entree.

18 baby eggplants	2 tablespoons chopped parsley
1 cup olive oil	18 small garlic cloves, peeled
3 medium onions, chopped finely	salt
7 ounces raisins	freshly ground pepper

Leave the eggplant whole, together with its green crown and a small piece of stem. Make a deep slit along the length of each eggplant and set aside. In a flameproof baking dish, large enough to hold the eggplants on one level, put 2 tablespoons of the olive oil and saute the chopped onion lightly. Add the raisins and chopped parsley; mix well together. Holding the eggplant slit up in your palm, stuff a bit of the onion and raisin mixture into each through the slit. Add a peeled clove of garlic in each. Return the eggplants to the baking dish and saute them lightly on all sides, turning carfully in order that the stuffing does not spill out. Turn them slit side up. Pour the remaining oil over, salt well, add a good grinding of pepper and bake in a 350° oven for 45 minutes. Serve hot or cold.

Serves 8.

Spinach and Rice
(Spinaka con Aroz)

With a bit of sauteed onion and rice, a pinch of sugar to bring out its flavor, and some lemon for balance, spinach becomes a worthy accompaniment for a roast or, filled out by a bowl of yoghurt, a lovely, light course in itself.

2 pounds spinach	½ cup rice
2 tablespoons olive oil	1 teaspoon salt
1 medium-sized onion, chopped finely	pinch of sugar
	juice of ½ lemon
¾ cup water	ground pepper

Wash and chop spinach and put in a colander to drain.

In a (lidded) pot, saute the chopped onion, uncovered, in the oil until transparent. Add the chopped spinach and mix with a wooden spoon. Add ¾ cup water, the rice, salt and sugar. Stir well, cover and cook gently until all the liquid is absorbed. Uncover, add the lemon juice and a grinding of pepper; mix in carefully. Taste, correct seasoning and serve.

Serves 6.

Stewed White Beans
(Yachini di Fijon Blanco)

Dried beans are a winter staple in most countries, and Bulgaria was no exception — only we ate them the year round. In this version, the beans are stewed with a variety of vegetables, a bay leaf and generous quantities of allspice and peppercorns. Then they are finished off in a rich sauce made with sweet red and green peppers and tomatoes and perked up with generous quantities of fresh and dried mint. The novel flavor combination of allspice and mint mark this dish as authentically ours.

1 pound white beans	1 green pepper, seeded and cubed
1 onion, stuck with a clove	3 large ripe tomatoes, peeled,
1 carrot, whole	seeded, and chopped
1 celery stalk, with leaves	1 tablespoon tomato paste
1 teaspoon salt	1 teaspoon salt
1 bay leaf	½ teaspoon sugar
10 peppercorns	1 large bunch fresh mint, un-
5 allspice kernels	chopped, or 3 tablespoons dried
1½ teaspoons light vegetable oil	mint tied in a cheesecloth
1 onion, chopped finely	pepper
1 red pepper, seeded and cubed	

Soak the beans overnight. Drain, and put them into a large pot with cold water to cover by ⅓. Bring the water to a boil and cook for three minutes. Drain the beans and return them to the pot. Cover with the same amount of fresh hot water, add the onion with the clove, the carrot, celery, salt and the bay leaf, peppercorns and allspice kernels tied into a cheesecloth bag.

Bring again to a boil, lower the heat, cover and cook over a low heat for about 1½ hours, or until the beans are tender. Drain the beans and remove the bulky pieces of vegetable as well as the spice bag.

In a large skillet, heat the oil and saute the chopped onion until golden. Add the chopped peppers, cook for another few minutes. Add the chopped tomatoes, the tomato paste, a teaspoon of salt, sugar and the mint, and cook over a low flame for another 15 minutes. Remove the mint, and add the beans to the vegetables in the skillet. Mix well, sprinkle in more mint if you have it fresh, correct the seasoning, add a good grinding of black pepper, and stew for another 10 minutes. Serve hot or cool.

Serves 6.

Baked White Beans
(Eijon Blanco al Orno)

A simpler, less saucy dish than the previous, this bean casserole, is just as gratifying. The paprika and allspice bake into the beans to give them a full-bodied flavor and rich, spicy aroma.

Hint: precooking the beans for a few minutes expels much of their gaseous quality and saves a lot of bother for people who suffer from bean bloat.

1 pound dried white beans	1½ teaspoons salt
1 onion with clove stuck in it	3 tablespoons tomato puree
1 bay leaf	pinch of sugar
10 peppercorns	2 tablespoons paprika
5 allspice kernels	

Wash and soak beans overnight. Drain.

Put the beans into a large pot, cover by ⅓ with cold water, bring to a boil, cook for three minutes and drain. Replace the beans in the casserole with the same amount of fresh hot water, add the onion with the clove, bay leaf, peppercorns and allspice all tied up in a cheesecloth. Add the salt and cook for 1½ hours or until tender. Uncover. Remove the spice bag and add tomato puree and a pinch of sugar. Mix well and spread into an oiled earthenware baking dish. Sprinkle with paprika and bake in a 350° oven until a crust forms, about ¾ hour.

Serves 6.

Stewed Yellow Beans
(Yachni di Fijon Amariyo)

These yellow wax beans, perked up with the piquant flavor of lemon and dill and a dash of sugar, are an excellent accompaniment to chicken and veal. So dainty themselves, they don't overpower the delicate tasting meats, while they add an eye-catching glint of spring color.

2 pounds fresh yellow wax beans	½ cup water
1 onion, finely chopped	1 tablespoon flour dissolved in 2
2 tablespoons light vegetable oil	tablespoons water
1 teaspoon salt	juice of ½ lemon
¼ teaspoon sugar	2 tablespoons chopped dill

Wash and string the yellow beans. Cut in half.

Chop and saute the onion in the oil until golden. Add the beans, salt, sugar and ½ cup water. Cook until almost tender, 20–30 minutes, depending upon the freshness of the beans. In a small bowl, dissolve the flour in 2 tablespoons of water, add the lemon juice and chopped dill and pour over beans. Cook for another 10 minutes. Taste, correct seasoning if necessary and serve.

An excellent accompaniment to all chicken and veal dishes.

Serves 6.

Stewed Green Beans
(Yachni di Fijon Verde)

The bean I like best is the green string bean, plentiful in America as well as Europe and available the year around. In Bulgaria we used a rather broad variety that was striated with little black lines, but the slender or any other kind of green bean is also very tasty. Though they lend themselves to countless transformations, we usually stewed them with onions and tomatoes, added a bit of sugar to perk up the flavors and served them as an accompaniment to meat or with yoghurt as a course in themselves.

2 pounds string beans, sliced diagonally
2 tablespoons light vegetable oil
1 onion, coarsely chopped
1 large tomato, peeled, seeded and coarsely chopped

¼ cup water
1 teaspoon salt
¼ teaspoon sugar
yoghurt (optional)

Wash, string and slice the beans. Heat the oil in a deep lidded pot, add the onion and tomato and cook gently, uncovered, for a few minutes. Add the beans, ¼ cup water, salt and sugar. Cover and simmer until tender, about 20 minutes or more. Uncover, correct seasoning, and serve hot or cold, with yoghurt on the side.

Serves 6.

Golden Potatoes with Onions
(Kartofis con Sivoya)

Potatoes and onions always make a tasty team. In this version, precooked potatoes and onions are sauteed separately to a light golden color, arranged on a platter and sprinkled generously with red paprika. For the surest results, use the large Idaho potatoes and yellow onions, as these keep their shape best. Goes wonderfully with grills and kebabs.

1½ pounds potatoes	1 teaspoon salt
2 large onions, sliced in rings	1 teaspoon paprika
3–4 tablespoons olive oil	

Boil potatoes on a low heat in their jackets until just cooked. Allow to cool, peel and slice.

In a large skillet heat the oil and saute the onions until soft and golden. Remove with a slotted spoon and reserve.

Add the potatoes to the skillet and saute them until light golden turning frequently. Don't worry if they break up.

Arrange the potatoes on a serving dish, spread the onions on top, add salt and the paprika, sprinkled across the top.

Serves 6.

Stewed Potatoes
(Yachni di Kartofis)

Potatoes form the main component of this uncommonly good vegetable stew. After sauteeing and stewing, the vegetables are joined in a baking dish and bound together with a handful of chopped parsley or dill. Makes a first-rate side dish or, with only a simple green salad, a one-course supper.

2 pounds potatoes
2 tablespoons light vegetable oil
2 onions, coarsely chopped
2 red or green peppers, seeded and coarsely chopped
1 stalk celery, chopped coarsely
3 ripe tomatoes, peeled, seeded and chopped

1 bay leaf
1 teaspoon salt
1 cup water
ground pepper
2 tablespoons chopped fresh parsley or dill

Wash, peel and quarter the potatoes. Put aside in a bowl of cold water.

Put the oil into a large skillet (with lid) and fry, uncovered, the chopped onions lightly. Add the peppers, chopped celery stalk and tomatoes. Cover, and cook for 10 minutes. Drain the potatoes and add them to the skillet. Add the bay leaf, salt and a cup of water. Cover and cook slowly until the potatoes are tender, about ½ hour. Uncover, add a grinding of pepper and the chopped parsley or dill. Remove to a 350° oven and bake for another 15 minutes.

Serves 8.

Stewed Red Cabbage
(Yachni di Kol Kolrada)

Widespread as the combination is, we tend to associate red cabbage and apples with Germany. But there's no underestimating the magic wrought by the zestful addition of both orange and lemon juice. This citrus-flavored dish goes splendidly with poultry, especially duck.

3 tablespoons light vegetable oil	juice of 1 orange
1 onion, chopped coarsely	1 teaspoon salt
1 red cabbage, shredded	1 tablespoon sugar
1 large tart apple, peeled, cored and sliced	3 tablespoons lemon juice or plain vinegar

In a lidded large skillet or heavy pot, melt the chopped onion in the oil. Add the shredded cabbage and cook over a low heat for a few minutes, mixing with a wooden spoon. Add the sliced apple, the orange juice, salt and sugar. Cover and cook for 15 minutes.

Remove the cover, add lemon juice (or vinegar). Taste, and correct seasoning. Cover again and continue cooking until done, around 40–50 minutes. Serve with roast duck or chicken.

Serves 6.

Cabbage with Rice
(Kol con Aroz)

This may be proof of the old adage that the simplest foods are also the best. We children were often served this quick-to-prepare peasant dish when there was no time to stuff the cabbage. With a pique of lemon it's remarkably fresh tasting and an excellent accompaniment to turkey.

2 tablespoons light vegetable oil
1 onion, chopped coarsely
1 green cabbage head, shredded
1 tomato, peeled, seeded and chopped
1 teaspoon salt
¼ teaspoon sugar

¼ cup water
¾ cup boiling water
½ cup rice
juice of 1½ lemons
ground pepper
ground cumin (optional)

In a deep pot with a lid, heat the oil and saute the onion, uncovered, until transparent. Add the cabbage, continue cooking for 5 minutes, stirring with a wooden spoon. Add the tomato, the salt, sugar and ¼ cup water, cover and cook for another 15 minutes. Uncover, add another ¾ cup boiling water and the rice. Cover again, and cook over a low heat until all the water is absorbed, about 10–12 minutes. Uncover, add the lemon juice, and plenty of freshly ground pepper and a sprinkling of ground cumin. Excellent with roast turkey.

Serves 6.

Sweet and Sour Onions
(Sivoikas Agras Dulces)

It takes a bit of time and patience to peel the small onions. But these sweet and sour delights are well worth the trouble. They are ideal with a roast, especialy roast lamb. If you can't find shallots, a rarity in some areas, baby onions can be bought in spring.

2 pounds shallots, or baby onions, 1 inch in diameter	juice of 1 lemon
2 tablespoons oil	2–3 tablespoons water
3 tablespoons sugar	½ teaspoon salt

Peel and blanch the onions in boiling water for 10 minutes. Drain. In a large lidded pan, heat the oil, add the sugar and allow it to turn light brown. Add the onions. Shake the pan and when the onions are nicely glazed, add the lemon juice and 2–3 tablespoons water. Add the salt, another pinch of sugar, cover and cook for 7–8 minutes. Taste, correct seasoning and serve as accompaniment to a roast of any kind.

Serves 6.

Pilaf of Tomatoes and Peppers
(Aroz con Domates i Pipiritzas)

We often cooked vegetables with rice to absorb the liquid of the vegetables and to make the rice more interesting. The red, green and white of this dish happens to correspond to the colors of the Bulgarian flag, though there are better reasons for enjoying it.

3 tablespoons light vegetable oil	1 teaspoon salt
1 pound onions, chopped coarsely	¼ teaspoon sugar
3 green peppers, seeded and chopped coarsely	1½ cups long-grained rice
3 tomatoes, peeled, seeded and chopped coarsely	2 tablespoons chopped dill or parsley
1½ cups water	½ teaspoon ground white pepper

In a large, flameproof casserole, heat the oil and lightly saute the onions. Add the peppers and continue cooking for three more minutes. Add the chopped tomatoes and cook another 5 minutes.

Add the water, salt and sugar. Cover and bring to a boil. Uncover, add the rice, lower the flame and spread a clean absorbent towel across the top of the casserole. Put on the lid, and cook until the water has been absorbed, about 18 minutes.

Uncover and fluff the rice with two forks. Add the parsley or dill and plenty of ground white pepper. Allow to rest 5 minutes before serving. Serve with a green salad.

Serves 8.

Stuffed Grape Leaves
(Yaprakes)

Greek in origin, *yaprakes* are at their best when made with the fresh leaves of the young vine. Lacking a vineyard, you can usually find them in brine at a Greek or Mideastern specialty shop. This version, filled with rice and cooked in a piquant dill and lemon sauce, with salt, pepper and a pinch of sugar, is lighter than the one with meat (see p. 115). It can also be eaten cold, with yoghurt. And if you want to alter the character of the dish entirely, you can simply substitute fresh mint for the dill.

30 tender grapevine leaves, fresh, or preserved in brine	**The Sauce:**
¼ cup olive oil	1 cup cold water
2 onions, chopped finely	juice of 1 lemon
¾ cup rice	1 teaspoon salt
1 teaspoon salt	1 teaspoon pepper
½ teaspoon ground pepper	¼ teaspoon sugar
2 tablespoons chopped fresh dill	2 tablespoons chopped dill
3 tablespoons water	yoghurt

Brined leaves should be thoroughly washed before using. If fresh vine leaves are used, blanch in hot water for a minute or two and drain.

In a skillet heat 2 tablespoons of the oil and saute the chopped onion until transparent. Add the rice, cook until it turns translucent, add salt, pepper and the chopped dill. Mix well. Add 3 tablespoons water to the mixture and as soon as it is absorbed, remove from heat. This is the mixture for filling.

In the center of each vine leaf put 1 teaspoonful of the filling and make a little parcel by folding up, first the stem end and then the sides. Roll them very tightly and squeeze closed. Arrange in one or two layers in a large shallow pan. In a small bowl, mix 1 cup water, the lemon juice, salt, pepper, sugar and the chopped dill. Pour over the stuffed vine leaves, press a plate down over the top to hold them in place and cook very gently for about an hour. Serve hot or cold with yoghurt.

Serves 8–10.

Stuffed Peppers
(Pipiritzas Ienas con Aroz)

In the Sephardic kitchen, vegetables are usually stuffed with raw rice, which fluffs to just the right texture when properly cooked. The best rice for the purpose is the long-grained variety, as it is less starchy than the others so the grains stay separate and chewy.

2 tablespoons light vegetable oil
2 onions, chopped finely
2 carrots, grated
1 celery stalk, chopped finely
1 cup rice
2 ripe tomatoes, peeled, seeded and chopped
1 teaspoon salt
½ teaspoon pepper
2 tablespoons chopped fresh dill
½ cup water
4 green peppers, whole with crowns and seeds removed

4 red peppers, whole with crowns and seeds removed

The sauce:
2 tablespoons tomato paste, mixed with 1 cup water
2 tablespoons light vegetable oil
pinch of sugar
1 teaspoon salt
½ teaspoon pepper
3 celery stalks, whole with leaves
2 tablespoons chopped fresh dill

Heat 2 tablespoons of the oil in a skillet, and saute the onions lightly. Add the grated carrots, and the single chopped celery stalk, and cook for a few minutes.

Mix in the rice and cook until it becomes transparent. Remove from heat. Add the chopped tomato, salt, pepper, chopped dill and half cup water. Mix well. Wash the peppers and remove crowns and seeds. Drain.

Stuff the peppers ¾ full with the rice mixture, leaving room for the rice to swell.

In a flameproof casserole, large enough to hold the peppers in one layer pour the tomato paste mixed with a cup of water. Add the remaining oil, a pinch of sugar, salt and a good grinding of pepper. Cook for 2–3 minutes.

Put the 3 whole celery stalks into the sauce on the bottom of the casserole and add the peppers upright in between, pushing them closely together. Cover with foil or a lid, and cook over a low heat for ½ hour. Uncover, add another generous sprinkling of chopped dill and finish cooking in a 350° oven for another half hour.

Serves 8.

SAVORY PIES, PASTRIES AND PASTAS

Pies, Pastries and Pastas

Savory pastries and pasta dishes are an intrinsic part of Sephardic cooking. Square, round, or triangular, large pies or small pastries, filled with chicken or beef, cheese or vegetables, fruit or jam — confections made with dough almost always appeared on our menu. They make marvelous hors d'oeuvres and desserts, interesting appetizers and buffet dishes, light meals and party delights.

Back home, every cook had her own little trick to make the dough more delicate and better tasting. My grandmother, for example, never measured, but her fingers knew exactly how much flour, water and fat to use. I, after experimenting over a long period of time, have arrived at measurements which satisfy me. Naturally, there are always slight variations depending on the moisture in the flour, the humidity in the air, and other circumstances — and this is where your own judgment might come into play. But for the beginning my guidelines, I think, are safe.

I include in this section five popular doughs and fillings best fitted to each. But the variations are endless, and there is every reason to experiment with your own combinations. In case you feel that you'd like to spread out the work, these doughs can be made in advance and kept frozen either before or after baking. But, for the right, substantial taste be sure to use plain white flour — unbleached.

There are also a number of recipes for dishes using the paper-thin fila dough, which can be purchased in any Greek or Mideastern specialty shop, and which is so difficult to make that I haven't included it in the five representative types. And, lastly, there are various and sundry pasta dishes. all easy to prepare and unpretentious.

A Simple Pastry Dough
(Masa Mal Tomada)

Refrigerating the dough before rolling makes it easier to handle by eliminating elasticity and shrinkage.

This dough can be used with all kinds of savory fillings, as in the recipe on p. 158. It should be made a day in advance.

2½ cups flour	1 tablespoon vinegar
½ teaspoon salt	⅓ cup cold water
1 cup margarine or butter	

Sift the flour and salt into a mixing bowl. Cut the fat into the flour in a food processor or with a pastry blender or two knives, until the mixture is amalgamated and grainy. It should feel like cornmeal or cream of wheat. Pour the vinegar and water into a bowl and mix in the dough mixture. Working quickly with your hands, blend all the flour with the liquid and shape it into a ball. Don't work the mixture; that makes it less light. Simply gather it together and pat it into a ball. Put into a plastic bag and let it rest for at least overnight in the refrigerator.

Fine Dough
(Masa Fina)

As the name suggests, this is a delicate, silky dough. It can used equally well for savory and sweet pies.

2½ cups flour	¼ cup safflower oil
1 teaspoon salt	1 tablespoon vinegar
½ cup margarine or butter,	¼ cup soda water (seltzer)
softened to room temperature	

Sift flour and salt onto a board and make a well in the center. Place the softened margarine (or butter) and oil in the well. Quickly and lightly, with the tips of your fingers, blend the flour into the margarine and oil. Mix the vinegar with the soda water and add it to the flour mixture. Work the mixture into a ball without kneading.

Place in a plastic bag and allow to rest for an hour in the refrigerator before using.

Flaky Dough
(Masa Afrijaldada)

If I have to label it, I would say this is a semi- or not-so-very-puffy puff pastry. It's especially good for cheese pies.

2½ cups flour	3 tablespoons sour cream
½ teaspoon salt	1 egg
1 cup margarine or butter, softened to room temperature	

The ingredients should be at room temperature when you begin.

Sift the flour and salt onto a board and make a well in the center. Place the margarine, sour cream and unwhipped egg in the well. Lightly, with the tips of your fingers, blend the flour into the fat and liquid. Knead gently for one minute and form a ball. Put in a plastic bag and allow to rest in the refrigerator an hour before using.

Sour Cream Dough
(Otra Masa Afrijaldada)

A variant of the preceding, delicate and light.

2½ cups flour	¼ cup margarine
½ teaspoon salt	1 cup sour cream

Sift flour and salt into a mixing bowl, cut the margarine into the flour in a food processor or with a pastry blender or two knives, until it resembles coarse meal. Add the sour cream. Mix until just bound and form into a ball. Put into a plastic bag, and let stand at least 6 hours in the refrigerator before using.

Noodle Dough
(Fila Pur Fideos)

Traditionally, this dough was kneaded by hand to a smooth and silky consistency. Today the process can be nicely handled in a matter of minutes with a food processor. The drying, however, still takes a day or two.

2 cups flour	1 tablespoon olive oil
½ teaspoon salt	2 tablespoons water
4 eggs	

Sift the flour and salt onto a board and make a well in the center. Place the unmixed eggs, oil and water into the well. Mix into a mass and put the mass into the food processor to knead for a minute or two with the plastic blade, or blend by hand into a workable mass and knead until silky and rubbery (about 10 minutes). Remove to a floured surface. Form a ball and then roll out very thinly. To shape the noodles, allow the dough to dry very slightly, for about ½ hour. Roll up the sheet loosely, and slice through the roll with a sharp knife into thin noodle strips. Put the rolled-up noodles on a dry towel to rest and dry for a day or two.

Spinach Pie
(Inchusa di Spinaka con Masa Mal Tomada)

A classic Sephardic dish featuring one of our most widely used vegetables. For success, thoroughly dry the spinach before chopping. Back home, it was washed, drained in a colander, chopped, spread out on a large platter and placed in the sun. Only then was it considered dry enough to go into the pie. If you use frozen spinach (which I don't recommend!) squeeze out all the water.

¾ pound fresh spinach
¾ cup white feta cheese, crumbled
¾ cup cream cheese
¼ cup hard mild katchkeval cheese, grated
4 eggs
½ teaspoon salt

1 portion *masa mal tomada*, the simple dough recipe on p. 153
1 egg white, lightly beaten
sesame seeds, to sprinkle (optional)
12-inch pie pan
yoghurt (or sour cream)

Wash spinach, and squeeze in a towel or in a salad spinner, to dry. Chop finely and leave to dry further in a colander.

In a large mixing bowl, blend together gently the cheeses and four whole eggs. Add the salt, and mix the spinach in well. Set aside while you roll the dough.

Roll out the dough and line a well-buttered 12-inch pie pan with half, leaving a small overhanging margin. Spread the spinach mixture evenly and cover the pie with the remaining dough. Seal the two layers of dough by pinching the edges together. Brush the top with slightly beaten egg white and sprinkle with sesame seeds (or, if not available, more grated katchkeval). Bake in preheated 350° oven until light golden, about 40–45 minutes. Serve with yoghurt or sour cream.

Ground Beef Pie
(Pastel di Karne con Masa Fina)

There are so many versions of meat-filled pastries that I can't begin to count. In South America, I know, raisins are added to produce a sweetish taste. In my family, we put in a small baked and chopped eggplant which gives an interesting twist to the meat mixture.

1 small eggplant	1 egg
1 onion, chopped finely	1 portion *masa fina* dough (p. 154)
1 pound lean beef, ground	1 egg yolk
2 tablespoons chopped parsley	1 tablespoon water
1 teaspoon salt	12-inch pie pan
½ teaspoon ground pepper	

Grill the eggplant whole over an open flame, if available, or under the broiler until blackened and soft. Allow to cool only to the point where you can pull off skin, place in a colander to drain. When it is drained of its juices, chop finely.

In a heavy frying pan, saute the chopped onion in the oil until it is transparent. Add the ground meat. Breaking the meat with a fork, saute just until the meat loses its redness. Add the chopped eggplant, chopped parsley, salt, pepper, whole egg. Mix well and set aside.

Grease a 12-inch pie pan, roll out half of the *masa fina* and line the pan, retaining a narrow overhang of dough. Spread the filling evenly. Roll out the remaining dough and cover the pie. Seal the pie by pinching the edges together. Brush the top with egg yolk which has been slightly beaten with 1 tablespoon water and prick the top all over with the tines of a fork.

Bake in 350° oven until light brown, about 40 minutes.

Leek Pie
(Inchusa di Prasa con Masa Fina)

I was very surprised to find in France *torte au Boriaux*, which for me meant a good old *inchusa di prasa*, and I must say a great favorite of mine. Katch-keval is a local Bulgarian cheese, which, if you can't find it, may be best replaced with a somewhat sharp, salty yellow cheese.

3 pounds leeks (after green tops are removed)
1 large onion, thinly sliced
4 tablespoons butter
1 cup sweet cream
½ cup katchkeval cheese, grated
3 eggs

1 portion *masa fina* dough (p. 154)
1 egg yolk
1 tablespoon water
salt and freshly ground pepper
12-inch pie pan

Clean and cut the leeks into 3 inch pieces, discarding the tough green upper parts. Put the leeks and sliced onion together in a saucepan, cover with cold water and bring to a boil. Boil the leeks and onions for ½ hour and drain. Shred the vegetables with a fork as they are draining. Melt the butter in a frying pan and saute the shredded vegetables for 5 minutes.

In a large mixing bowl, mix the sweet cream, grated katchkeval and eggs. Mix well and add the sauted vegetables. Mix again and set aside.

Roll out the *masa fina* dough and line the buttered pie tin with half of the dough, leaving a small margin overhanging. Spread the leek filling evenly and cover with the remaining dough, sealing the edges. Brush with egg yolk mixed with 1 tablespoon water and pierce the top with the tines of a fork. Bake in 375° oven until light golden, about 40 minutes.

Cheese Tartlets
(Kezadas di Ceso con Masa Afrijaldada)

A little hors d'oeuvre to begin the meal. Traditionally *kezadas* were shaped by hand. My grandmother could mold little rounds of dough into delicately fluted pastry shells, fill them, seal them, and make each one look exactly like the next. Because I can't, I advise using muffin tins.

1 portion *masa afrijaldada*, the flaky dough on p. 155	2 whole eggs, lightly beaten
¼ cup butter	½ pound katchkeval cheese, grated
2 tablespoons flour	½–1 teaspoon salt
2 cups milk	½ teaspoon freshly ground nutmeg
	muffin tins

On a floured surface, roll out the dough into a quarter-inch-thick rectangle. With a dough cutter or drinking glass, cut out rounds large enough to line the muffin tins to the rim.

Butter the muffin tins. Place each dough circle in the tin and press the dough around the sides to cover the cup completely. Prick the bottom with the tines of a fork. Place in refrigerator while you fix the filling.

In a large saucepan, melt the butter. Blend in the flour, and when it has amalgamated into the butter, slowly begin to add the milk, mixing all the while to prevent lumping. Bring to the boiling point and remove from heat.

Add the lightly beaten eggs and grated cheese. Taste for seasoning and add salt and a good grinding of nutmeg. Blend well. Spoon the mixture into the dough-lined muffin tins to about three-quarters full, and bake in a 375° oven until the tarts are puffed and golden (about ½ hour).

Run a thin knife around the edge to remove. Serve immediately.

Makes 24 tartlets.

Little Eggplant Pies
(Kezadas di Merendjena con Masa Afrijaldada)

These delicate little pies make the perfect hors d'oeuvre to serve with drinks. When serving them, I eliminate a first course.

1 portion *masa afrijaldada*, the flaky dough recipe on p. 155
1 large or 2 small eggplants
½ cup feta cheese, crumbled

⅓ cup katchkeval cheese, grated
½ teaspoon salt
2 whole eggs, lightly beaten
muffin tins

Roll out the dough into a quarter-inch-thickness. With a pastry cutter or drinking glass, cut out round shapes to fit into the muffin tins. Butter the muffin tins and place in each cup a circle of dough. Press around the sides until each muffin cup is lined completely with dough. Place in refrigerator while you prepare the filling.

Grill the eggplant under a broiler, or over a flame (if available), until it is black all over and soft inside. Remove to a board, and when the eggplant is cool, peel off the skin and place in a colander to drain for half an hour. This removes the bitter juice.

Chop the eggplant finely, put it in a mixing bowl and add the crumbled feta cheese, ¼ cup of the katchkeval, salt and the lightly beaten eggs. Mix well.

Fill the dough-lined muffin tins with the eggplant-cheese mixture until three-quarters full. Sprinkle each tartlet with the remaining katchkeval cheese, and bake in a 375° oven until puffed and slightly golden, about 30 minutes.

Run a sharp knife around the edge and remove. Should be served hot.

Makes 24.

Cheese Pie
(Inchusa di Ceso con Otra Masa Afrijaldada)

I have included three kinds of cheese, katchkeval, cream, and feta, each with a very different flavor and consistency. But you can make your own substitutions. It's fun to experiment. With a salad, this pie is a satisfying midday meal, excellent for luncheons.

1 portion *otra masa afrijaldada*, the sour cream dough on page 156
¾ cup feta cheese
¾ cup cream cheese
¾ cup katchkeval cheese, grated
1 potato, peeled, boiled soft and mashed
½ teaspoon salt
½ teaspoon pepper
½ teaspoon freshly ground nutmeg
5 eggs, whole
1 egg white, lightly beaten
sesame seeds for sprinkling on top (optional)
12-inch pie pan

In a mixing bowl, blend well the feta cheese, cream cheese and grated katchkeval. Mix in mashed potato, the salt and a good grinding of both pepper and nutmeg. Beat in the 5 whole eggs, one by one. Set aside. Roll out the dough and line a well-buttered 12-inch pie tin with half. Spread the filling evenly. Cover with the rest of the dough and seal the pie by pinching the sides together. Brush with lightly beaten egg white. Score with a fork and sprinkle with sesame seeds. Bake in a 375° oven until puffed and golden, about 45 minutes.

163

Puffed Cheese Triangles
(Shamizikos di Fila con Ceso)

Fila is a dough better purchased than attempted, and these days is easy to find in a Mideastern or Greek specialty store. If you don't find it easily, strudel dough can be substituted.

Filling:	Dough:
½ cup cream cheese	8 sheets prepared fila dough
½ cup katchkeval cheese, grated	6 tablespoons oil
2 eggs, lightly beaten	½ cup butter
½ teaspoon salt	
½ teaspoon ground nutmeg	

Prepare the filling: mix the cheeses together. Beat in the eggs and add the salt and nutmeg.

In a small skillet, melt the butter with the oil. Remove from heat. Separate the fila dough and cut each sheet into long strips of 2 inches width. Brush each strip with the butter and oil mixture.

To arrange the triangles, put one tablespoon of filling on the bottom of each strip. Fold one corner of the bottom of the strip over to the opposite side, beginning a triangle. You can practice with a strip of paper before beginning. In this way you can see best where to place the filling and how to roll it up tightly.

Make sure the filling stays within the dough. Bring the opposite corner up to continue the triangular folding, and continue folding in this way until you reach the end of the strip. You should now have a small triangular package. Finish all the strips in this manner. These are your *shamizikos*.

Put the *shamizikos* on a well-buttered sheet, brush the tops with the remainder of the oil-butter mixture, and bake in a preheated 400° oven until golden and crisp, about 20 minutes. Serve hot.

Chicken-Filled Pastry Triangles (Shamizikos di Fila con Karne di Picadura di Pujo)

These little chicken-filled triangular pastries go beautifully with a hot soup in winter or a cold one in summer. They also make tasty and elegant hors d'oeuvres.

1 onion, chopped finely	½ teaspoon ground pepper
½ pound ground chicken breast	2 tablespoons chopped fresh dill
2 tablespoons light vegetable oil	1 egg, lightly beaten
1 tablespoon fresh bread crumbs	8 sheets prepared fila dough
1 teaspoon salt	vegetable oil for coating

In a frying pan, saute the onion until soft. Add the ground chicken breast and continue to saute the meat until it turns white. Remove from heat. Add the bread crumbs, salt, ground pepper and chopped dill. Bind with the lightly beaten egg and allow to cool.

Separate the fila sheets and cut each sheet into long, 2-inch-wide strips. Place a tablespoon of filling at one end of the sheet. Bring up one corner of the sheet over to the opposite side, beginning a triangle shape. Make sure the filling stays inside the dough. Bring the other corner up and continue to fold from either side until you finish the strip. You should now have a little triangular package.

Lay the triangles on a baking sheet, coat with vegetable oil and bake in a 400° oven about 20–25 minutes, until puffed and golden.

Cheese-Filled Pastry
(Frijalda di Ceso)

Fila dough crumbles like crisp autumn leaves when you bite into it, and is a perfect enclosure for a succulent cheese filling. The loaves should be served straight out of the oven, when the pastry has puffed up just right and the egg and milk mixture turned golden.

⅔ cup butter	½ teaspoon ground nutmeg
¼ cup safflower oil	12 sheets prepared fila dough
¾ cup feta cheese	1½ cups milk
⅔ cup katchkeval cheese, grated	14-inch square shallow baking
4 eggs, whole	pan, buttered
½ teaspoon salt	

Melt the butter and oil together in a skillet. Set aside.

In a mixing bowl blend the cheeses well and add two of the eggs. Add the salt and nutmeg and mix again. Separate the fila sheets and spread out a first layer of fila on a clean towel. Brush the sheet with the oil-butter mixture. Place a second layer of fila directly on top of the first, brush again with oil-butter, and top it with a third layer of fila.

Divide the cheese mixture into four portions, and distribute one portion in little 1-inch mounds across the top of the three layers of fila.

Using the towel underneath, roll the layers lightly to form a loaf. Carefully place along one side of the buttered baking pan. Make three additional loaves in the same way, using all the fila and cheese. Place each loaf one next to the other in the baking pan, pressing them in if the fit is tight. Bake in a preheated 350° oven for 20–25 minutes until the pastry begins to turn golden.

While the *frijalda* is baking, beat the remaining 2 eggs into the milk. When the pastry begins to turn golden, after 20–25 minutes, remove it from the oven, prick the surface lightly with a fork, pour the milk mixture over the pastry and return to the oven for approximately 10 more minutes until light golden.

Bring to the table in the baking pan and serve in broad slices.

166

Brain-Filled Pastry Loaves
(Mina di Miyoyo)

An exotic, sophisticated dish that sounds more complicated to prepare than it is.

The Filling:
2 calves' brains
2 tablespoons vinegar
salt
1 bay leaf
5 peppercorns, whole

3 eggs, lightly beaten
1 teaspoon salt
½ teaspoon ground pepper
½ teaspoon ground nutmeg
2 tablespoons chopped dill

The Bechamel:
2 tablespoons margarine
2 tablespoons flour
¾ cup chicken broth

For preparation:
10 sheets prepared fila dough
5 tablespoons margarine
5 tablespoons light vegetable oil
12-inch square baking tin

Soak the brains in a small bowl of water acidulated with 1 tablespoon vinegar for an hour. Drain. Remove the film and membranes from the brains and discard them. Cook brains in another pan of salted water acidulated with the second tablespoon of vinegar as well as the bay leaf and peppercorns, for about 10 minutes.

Remove from liquid and allow to cool. Cut into small, ½ inch cubes. Prepare the bechamel, melt the margarine, and blend in the flour. Add the chicken broth slowly. When it begins to thicken remove from heat and add the lightly beaten eggs, the salt, ground pepper, nutmeg and chopped dill. Add the cubed brains to the bechamel and mix well.

In a small saucepan, for the final preparation melt the margarine with the vegetable oil. Remove from heat. With a bit of the mixture, oil the bottom of the baking tin. Lay a layer of the fila leaves smoothly over the bottom and brush it with some of the oil-margarine mixture. Lay over another layer of fila dough and brush again with the oil and margarine. Lay over three more fila dough layers in this manner. Across the top of the fifth layer spoon the brain-bechamel mixture and spread evenly across the fila leaves. Lay over another fila sheet, tucking the edges down over the brain mixture. Brush with oil mixture. Lay over each of the remaining four fila sheets in this manner. With a sharp knife, pierce the upper layers, making large diamond designs. Oil lightly, still reserving some of the oil-margarine mixture.

Bake in a 375° oven for 10 minutes. Remove, and pour the remaining oil-margarine mixture into the ridges made by the scoring of the knife. Replace in oven and bake until puffed and golden, another 20–25 minutes.

Wrinkled Fila with Cheese
(Kalizones con Ceso)

Wrinkled fila is made by scrunching up the flat layer of dough with your fingertips — something like the way you might crumple a piece of paper — into a small mound about an inch high. The resulting dough is alternately crisp and chewy, and an absorbent, if unusual, receptacle for the melting cheese that seeps into it.

The Dough:
10 sheets prepared fila dough
⅓ cup butter
3 tablespoons safflower oil

The Filling:
¾ cup feta cheese, crumbled
¾ cup cream cheese

⅔ cup katchkeval cheese

The Topping:
3 eggs, lightly beaten
1 cup milk
1 teaspoon salt
½ teaspoon ground pepper
12-inch square baking pan

In a small saucepan, melt the butter with the oil. Remove from heat. Oil the bottom of the baking pan with a bit of the mixture. On a flat dish lay out a single layer of fila and brush with the oil-butter mixture. Wrinkle up the fila into a small pile about an inch high at its top and 2½ inches diameter and place in the baking pan. Oil another layer of fila and make a small wrinkled pile next to the first. Cover the bottom of the baking pan in this way; it should take five fila leaves. If there are spaces in between, spread the edges of the wrinkled piles to cover completely the bottom of the dish.

In a mixing bowl, blend the cheeses. Spread half the cheese mixture as best you can across the top of the gathered fila leaves. Oil and wrinkle each of the remaining fila leaves and place them across the top of the cheese mixture. Spread the remaining cheese mixture across the top.

Prick the surface all over with a fork. Beat the eggs, add the milk, the salt, nutmeg and pepper. Drip the mixture over the entire top of the fila leaves and bake in a 350° oven until golden, puffed and crisped, about 45 minutes. Serve warm.

Haman's Hair
(Vermicelli in Oil and Lemon Sauce)
(Caveos di Aman)

On Sabbath mornings after synagogue, we sat down to a glass of arak accompanied by *caveos di aman* and baked eggs. Today I serve it on a hot summer day with chilled roast beef or other cold cuts.

1 pound vermicelli (thinnest egg noodles)	½ teaspoon ground black pepper
juice of 2 lemons	about 15 black olives, pitted and halved
½ cup olive oil	3 hard-boiled eggs, quartered
1 teaspoon salt	

Boil a large pan of salt water, drop in the vermicelli and cook until just *al dente* (about 3 minutes). Drain.

While the noodles are cooking and draining, make a sauce of the lemon juice and oil, add the salt and pepper. Pour the sauce over the hot, drained vermicelli, and mix well. Allow to cool and serve garnished with black olives and wedges of hard-boiled eggs.

Serves 4.

Vermicelli with Fresh Tomatoes
(Fideos con Domates)

This isn't like any Italian pasta dish you've ever tasted, but it's one of my favorites with meatballs.

1 pound vermicelli (thinnest egg noodles)	3 tablespoons olive oil
	1 teaspoon salt
3 large ripe tomatoes, peeled, seeded and quartered	½ teaspoon freshly ground pepper

Boil a good amount of salted water and drop in the vermicelli for just two minutes. Drain the vermicelli, reserving the boiling water.

Boil the water again and drop in the tomatoes for half a minute. Drain and peel the tomatoes, squeezing out the seeds. Cut into quarters.

In a heavy frying pan, heat the oil and saute the tomato quarters for 5 minutes. Add the vermicelli, salt and ground pepper, mix well and cook for another 5 minutes until the vermicelli is cooked, stirring often to avoid sticking.

Serves 4.

Oven-Baked Noodles with Cheese and Cream
(Fideos con Ceso)

Sublimely creamy and rich, this single casserole dish is a meal in itself. Serve with a large, varied salad and crisp warm bread.

1 pound flat egg noodles (tagliatelli)	1 cup katchkeval cheese, grated
1½ cups sweet cream	½ teaspoon salt
	2 ounces butter

In a large pan of boiling salted water, cook the noodles until just *al dente*, still firm to the bite. Drain.

While the noodles are cooking, mix the cream and ¾ of the cheese together in a large mixing bowl. Add salt. When the noodles are drained, add them to the cream and cheese and mix well.

Spread the entire mixture in a buttered baking dish and dot the top with butter. Sprinkle the remaining ¼ of the grated katchkeval on top and bake in a 350° oven until golden, 25–30 minutes.

Serves 4–6.

Baked Macaroni and Cheese, Sephardic Style
(Macarones con Ceso)

My forefathers must have known something about the nouvelle cuisine. They used cream cheese rather than the bechamel sauce that the Italians used to blend the pasta and cheeses.

1 pound long macaroni noodles	⅓ cup katchkeval cheese, grated
4 eggs, lightly beaten	½ teaspoon salt
½ cup milk	½ teaspoon freshly ground pepper
¾ cup cream cheese	butter
¾ cup feta cheese, crumbled	shallow baking dish

Cook the macaroni in plenty of boiling salted water until just *al dente*, still firm to the bite. Drain.

Using an electric mixer, beat together lightly the eggs and milk. Add the cheeses, reserving 1 tablespoon of grated katchkeval. Add the salt and pepper.

Remove the bowl from the mixer and mix in the drained macaroni. Pour the entire mixture into a buttered baking dish. Dot with butter, sprinkle the remaining katchkeval on top and bake in a 350° oven until golden, about 30 minutes.

Serves 6.

Macaroni Moussaka
(Mussaka di Macarones)

Eggplant moussaka is a well-known dish. This is a variation featuring pasta.

1 pound long macaroni

Meat filling:
2 tablespoons light vegetable oil
1 large onion, coarsely chopped
1½ pounds lean ground beef
3 large tomatoes, peeled, seeded and chopped, or ½ cup tomato paste
1 teaspoon salt

1 teaspoon sugar
½ teaspoon ground pepper

Bechamel sauce:
3 tablespoons margarine
3 tablespoons flour
1½ cups chicken broth
3 eggs, lightly beaten
3 tablespoons chopped parsley

Cook the macaroni in plenty of boiling salted water until *al dente*, still firm to the bite. Drain. In a heavy frying pan, saute the onion in the oil until soft. Add the ground meat and cook until the meat loses its color. Add the peeled, seeded and chopped tomatoes (or tomato paste), salt and sugar. Lower the heat and cook for 15 minutes. Add the pepper.

In another saucepan prepare the bechamel. Melt the margarine and stir in the flour. When the two are amalgamated, add the chicken broth, mixing continuously to prevent lumps. When it begins to thicken, remove from heat. Add the lightly beaten eggs.

Line the bottom of an oiled baking dish with half the macaroni, spread half of the meat mixture over this, and top it with half of the bechamel sauce. Spread the second half of the macaroni, the meat mixture and the bechamel. Sprinkle with lots of parsley and bake in a 350° oven until golden and crisp, about 40–45 minutes.

Serves 6.

SALADS AND PICKLES

Salads and Pickles

Salads or pickles and sometimes both were almost invariably placed on the table along with the plates, glasses and cutlery. And it is as hard for me to remember a meal without one or the other as without the dinnerware.

Most of our salads are made with vegetables that have been at least partially cooked. Eggplants are grilled or fried, as are peppers, green beans, beetroot, and again peppers are parboiled; and white beans are cooked to softness before being dressed, seasoned, garnished and chilled for serving. And the few exceptions only prove the rule. Our cucumber salad is seeped in a vinegar marinade for several hours before serving, while in our mixed salad grilled peppers are added to the fresh cucumbers, tomatoes and onions. In consequence, many of our salads can, and some of them must, be prepared in advance; seeped in their vinegar or oil dressings, they tend to keep in the refrigerator for up to about a week. Their relative longevity, in contrast to the standard American lettuce, tomato and cucumber salad, which has to be brought to the table just as soon as it's ready, makes them very convenient.

Pickles, of course, keep even longer in the refrigerator, up to at least a month, to estimate conservatively. While they were eaten mostly in the winter, the summer months were filled with their preparation. I vividly remember my grandmother's tables covered with colorful vegetables laid out for shredding, cutting or quartering before they were to be pickled and deposited in the large wooden barrels in our cellar, from which we children could ecstatically help ourselves. Incidentally, the pickles were stored right next to the preserves, which had the habit of occasionally exploding their glass jars and scaring the daylights out of us.

From a culinary point of view, the cramped modern kitchen is a sorry loss, perhaps nowhere more unfortunate than in the matter of pickling. Needless to say, there is no resemblance whatsoever between homemade pickles and ones you buy in the store. But, admittedly, keeping them is problematic. In Israel, minus pantry and minus cellar, I stand a few wide-mouthed glass jars of my favorite pickles on a kitchen shelf, where they are easily accessible and highly decorative. But there is no place I have yet found to store one of the most common and delicious pickles of my youth: the whole pickled cabbage, whose leaves can be torn off and eaten separately or wrapped around a meat and rice stuffing. To my lasting regret, there is little point in including the recipe with the others.

176

Eggplant Salad (1)
(Salata di Mirindgena)

In this dish, the smokey flavor is the predominant one, perked up by lemon juice and finely chopped onion. Chilled, it makes an excellent first course or snack.

2 medium-sized eggplants	juice of ½ lemon (optional)
3 tablespoons olive oil	10 pitted black olives
1 teaspoon salt	½ small onion, chopped finely
pinch of sugar	

Grill the eggplants whole until they are completely black outside and soft inside. This can be done either atop the stove directly resting over an open flame, or under the grill of the broiler. Done in this way the skin imparts a smokey flavor to the pulp of the eggplant.

Remove the eggplants to a wooden board, and peel off the skin while they are still warm. Put in a colander. Allow them to drain off the juice for at least ½ hour. Chop the eggplant pulp into the bowl of an electric mixer, turn on the mixer at low speed and begin to add the oil slowly, blending until all the oil is used. Add salt and pinch of sugar (and the optional lemon juice). Chill. Garnish with black olives and serve with chopped onion separately.

Serves 6–8.

Eggplant Salad (2)
(Salata di Mirindgena)

This eggplant salad was usually prepared in summer, put in hermetically sealed containers and stored in the pantry to serve as a side dish all winter long. But it is just as good when served fresh.

2 medium-sized eggplants, weighing together about 2 pounds	3 garlic cloves, crushed
1 green pepper	salt
1 red pepper	pinch of sugar
1 large tomato, peeled, seeded and chopped	3 tablespoons wine vinegar
	¼ cup olive oil

Grill the eggplant and peppers over an open flame, if available, or under the broiler until they are black on all sides. The eggplants should be soft inside. Peel the eggplants while still warm and allow to drain off their inside juices for at least ½ hour. Chop finely into a medium-sized bowl.

Rub the blackened skin off the peppers, slice open, remove and discard seeds. Chop peppers finely. Add to the chopped eggplant pulp.

Peel the tomato by placing it in boiling water for a moment. Slice in half and squeeze out the seeds and juice. Chop finely and add to peppers and eggplant.

Mix the chopped vegetables well, add the crushed garlic, salt to taste and a pinch of sugar. Mix in the vinegar, then add the oil and taste again for seasoning. Store in a glass container until ready to serve. Serve with crackers or flat pitta bread. The salad will keep for a week in the refrigerator.

Serves 6–8.

Eggplant Fritters in Vinegar Sauce (Frittas di Mirindgenas con Sos di Vinagre)

These eggplants slices, fried and marinated in a vinegar sauce with dill and plenty of garlic, are for people who enjoy their vegetables strongly seasoned.

2 medium-sized eggplants, weighing together about 2 pounds	1 tablespoon water
2 eggs whites, lightly beaten until frothy	¼ teaspoon sugar
½ cup olive oil	salt to taste
3 tablespoons wine vinegar	4 tablespoons chopped fresh dill
	4–5 garlic cloves, crushed

Slice the eggplant into widthwise quarter-inch slices. Sprinkle each slice with salt and allow to drain for at least half an hour. Wash off the salt and pat dry.

Beat the egg whites until frothy but not stiff in a mixing bowl. In a heavy skillet, heat the oil. When the oil is sizzling hot, dip the eggplant slices in the egg whites and fry quickly until crisp. Drain on paper towels.

In a small bowl, mix the vinegar, water, sugar, salt, chopped dill and crushed garlic. Arrange eggplant on serving dish and spoon the vinegar mixture over it. Allow to stand for a few hours before serving. The eggplant slices will no longer be crisp, but rather permeated with the vinegar mixture.

Serves 6–8.

Beetroot Salad
(Salata di Tchukundur)

The Sephardic way of eating salad is usually as an accompaniment to the main course. Lightly pickled beet slices keep for at least a month and can be served as accompaniment to all kinds of *fritas* as well as chicken.

2 pounds beets	salt to taste
salted water to cook	pinch of sugar
1 cup red wine vinegar	¼ cup cumin seeds
1 cup water	

Wash the beetroot well without peeling and cook in a good amount of salted water until just tender.

Peel and slice the beetroots while they are still warm. Mix together the vinegar, water, salt, sugar and cumin seeds. Put the beetroot slices into a glass container or large bowl, pour the vinegar water mixture over the beets and allow to marinate in the refrigerator for one or two days before serving.

Serves 6–8.

Paprikas in Vinegar
(Gambas in Vinagre)

Gambas are the red, round peppers — almost resembling in shape a gardenia. Serve them in a glass bowl, with a bayleaf on the side and a few kernels of allspice. It is a beautiful dish.

2 pounds paprikas or sweet red peppers	2 tablespoons sugar
2 cups water	2 bay leaves
2 cups vinegar	10 peppercorns
1 tablespoon salt	10 (kernels) whole allspice

Wash the peppers whole and prick each one through with a fork 2 or 3 times. In a saucepan large enough to hold all the peppers, bring the water, vinegar, salt, sugar, bay leaves, peppercorns and allspice to a boil. One by one, add the peppers to the pan, bring again to the boil and cook for 5 minutes uncovered.

Remove the peppers with a slotted spoon, place in a glass container, and pour the liquid over them. Refrigerate for a few days before serving.

Serves 6–8.

Grilled Whole Peppers
(Pipiritzas Asadas)

Light green, dark green, red round, red long, yellow long are only a few of the many colors and shapes that peppers take. Choose according to taste and availability.

2 pounds green or red pepeprs, or a mixture of both
coarse salt

4 tablespoons vinegar
2 tablespoons light vegetable oil
½ teaspoon sugar

Grill the peppers whole atop the stove over an open flame (if available), or under the broiler, until they are completely black. (Turn slowly as each side becomes black.) Before peeling, put them in a shallow container or dish, sprinkle with coarse salt and cover. Let them sweat this way for at least an hour, and you'll find they peel easily and stay whole.

Peel, carefully slice away the green crowns and remove the seeds inside, without breaking up the pepper. This can be done by washing out the seeds under a gently flowing faucet. Place the peppers in a round, shallow serving dish, large enough to hold them all on a single level. Mix the vinegar, oil and sugar, pour over the peppers and store, covered, in a cool place for at least 3 hours.

Serves 6–8.

Grilled Pepper Salad
(Pipiritzas Asadas)

I like to mix red, green and yellow peppers for a colorful salad, but for taste any one of them will do. Unlike the previous two grilled pepper salads, this one is distinguished by the strong flavor of garlic.

2 pounds sweet peppers (red or green)	4 garlic cloves, crushed
1 teaspoon salt	3 tablespoons olive oil

Grill the peppers whole, either atop the stove over an open flame or under the broiler until black on all sides. (Turn slowly as each side becomes black.) Rub off the blackened skin from each, cut off the green crowns and slice in half lengthwise. Remove seeds. Slice each half lengthwise into one-inch strips. Place in shallow serving dish. Salt well, crush the garlic into the oil and pour over the peppers. Store covered in a cool place until ready to serve.

Serves 6–8.

Cucumber Salad
(Salata di Pipino)

This cucumber salad is probably of German or Austrian origin, and its arrival in Bulgaria and other parts of the world attests to the internationality of culinary art. Our version features garlic, rather than the grated onion that the Germans and Austrians use.

1 pound cucumbers	pinch of sugar
3 tablespoons white wine vinegar	good grinding of white pepper
¼ cup water	4 tablespoons chopped dill
½ teaspoon salt	3 garlic cloves, crushed

Peel the cucumbers and slice as thinly as possible into a large salad bowl. In a separate bowl, mix the vinegar, water, salt, sugar, white pepper and dill. Squeeze in the garlic. Mix well, and pour over the cucumbers. Mix again well. Let stand for a few hours in the refrigerator and serve chilled.

Serves 6.

Mixed Salad
(Salata Amestechada)

I don't think that there's a household in Sophia that didn't serve this mixed salad daily in the summer, when tomatoes, cucumbers and peppers were all plentiful and sweet. The combination of soft grilled peppers and crisp raw vegetables gives this salad its special flavor.

2 peppers (red or green)	salt
2 cucumbers, peeled and thinly sliced	pinch of sugar
	1 tablespoon light vegetable oil
2 tomatoes, thinly sliced	2 tablespoons vinegar
1 medium-sized onion, thinly sliced	2 tablespoons chopped parsley

Grill the peppers either atop the stove over an open flame or under the broiler until black on all sides. (Turn the peppers as they become blackened.) When cool, rub off the blackened skin, remove the stem and seeds, and slice into thin strips.

Combine all the vegetables in a salad bowl, add salt and sugar, oil and vinegar. Mix again, add the chopped parsley and serve.

Serves 6.

White Bean Salad
(Salata di Fijon Blanco)

You may be tempted to forgo the lengthy soaking and cooking and simply pour the olives and dressing over canned beans. But what you save in time you sacrifice in taste. Home cooked, this white bean salad is a most agreeable accompaniment to shishlik and kebab and a fine dish for a cold buffet.

1 pound dried white haricot beans	1 cup chopped onion
2 carrots, peeled and whole	½ cup wine vinegar
2 celery stalks, washed and halved	½ cup olive oil
1 onion, peeled	salt
2 bay leaves	freshly ground black pepper
10 peppercorns, whole	2 tablespoons chopped parsley
5 kernels allspice, whole	15 black olives
1 teaspoon salt	

Soak the beans in a large amount of water for at least 8 hours. Rinse and drain. Put the beans in a large saucepan with enough water to cover by half and bring slowly to a boil. Let them cook for 2 or 3 minutes, remove from heat and discard the cooking water. This helps to rid the beans of their gas. Return them to the pot and pour the same amount of hot water over the beans. Add the carrots, celery and onion to the pot. Tie the bay leaf, peppercorns and allspice into a small piece of cheesecloth, and add to the pot. Add salt, cover and cook over to a low to medium heat until the beans are soft, about 3 hours. Drain, remove the vegetables and the bag of spices, and pour the beans into a mixing bowl.

In a separate bowl, mix the chopped onion, vinegar, and oil. Pour the dressing over the beans. Add salt and a good grinding of black pepper, mix well again and leave to marinate for at least 2 hours. Sprinkle generously with parsley, garnish with the olives and serve.

Serves 8–10.

Green Bean Salad
(Salata di Fijon Vedre)

The most important thing to remember in this simple salad is not to overcook the beans. Five minutes or a little longer if the beans are tough is enough time to make them edible — but by all means they should remain crisp. Hot or cold, this salad is a perfect accompaniment to a summer meal and goes well with every type of meat.

2 pounds fresh green beans	3 tablespoons olive oil
1 tomato, seeded and coarsely chopped	2 tablespoons vinegar
	1½ teaspoons salt
1 small onion, thinly sliced and separated into rings	¼ teaspoon sugar
	parsley for garnish

Boil the beans whole, until they are cooked but still crisp, about 5 minutes. Rinse them in cold water, and allow to drain. Place the beans in a salad bowl, add the tomato and onion and mix all well.

In a separate container mix the oil, vinegar, salt and sugar. Just before serving, pour the dressing over the vegetables, mix well and sprinkle with parsley.

Serves 8.

Pickled Cabbage with Vegetables (Trushi di Kol)

Various kinds of pickled cabbage were a staple in our house, to be used in making stuffed cabbage (p. 118) and turkey with cabbage (p. 103), and as a regular accomapniment to many meat meals. This is one of our fancier versions, the cabbage being dressed up by celery, tomato, red pepper and carrots.

several large mason jars or other pickling jars
1 firm large cabbage head
3 carrots, scraped and sliced
2 stalks of celery, chopped, leaving leaves unchopped
1 large tomato, chopped

1 sweet red pepper, seeded and sliced
⅓ cup salt
6 cups water
12–15 sprigs of dill, whole
2–3 kernels allspice for each jar

Wash and cut the cabbage into quarters, cut out the core and slice thinly. In a large mixing bowl, mix the cabbage together with the other vegetables, the carrots, the celery stalks (excluding the leaves), the tomato and pepper. Sprinkle with a teaspoon of the salt, and rub it well into all the vegetables with the palms of your hands. In another bowl dissolve the remaining salt in 6 cups water.

Put the vegetables into the pickling jars, cover with the salted water, and top each jar with a large sprig or two of dill, some celery leaves and 2 or 3 kernels of allspice. Tie a piece of clean cheesecloth over the top of each jar. Put them in a warm, light place, Leave overnight. Next day, pour off the water from each jar — reserving the water — and taste the water for seasoning. It should not taste too salty, but it should be salty. Add water or salt if necessary. Return the water to the jars, cover again and store in a warm, light place. The pickling will be ready in 6–8 days, depending upon the season. (The vegetables pickle more quickly in the summer.) When pickled, remove cheesecloth, cover each with the original lid of the jar and store in a dark, cool place. It will keep for several weeks.

188

Pickled Cabbage
(Trushi di Kol)

Shredded cabbage pickled with dill and allspice served our family at practically every main meal. As a lady with a "sour tooth," I still prefer pickles to pastries for my secret snacks.

1 large, wide-mouthed glass jar or crock, large enough to hold the cabbages
2 small heads of cabbage
6 cups water
⅓ cup salt

4 celery stalks with their leaves
1 bunch dill (10–15 stalks fresh dill)
2 carrots, sliced
5 kernels allspice

Wash and quarter the cabbage heads without removing the core. Pour the water into a mixing bowl and dissolve the salt into it. Cover the bottom of the glass jar or crock with celery leaves. Arrange over them the cabbage quarters, alternating with sprigs of dill, celery and pieces of carrot, pushing all down together in the jar. Add the allspice and fill the jar with the salted water. Top with celery and dill sprigs and cover the top with a piece of cheesecloth. Let the jar stand in a warm, light place for 4–6 days. Remove the cheesecloth, cover the jar with lid or foil and store in cool dark place. It will keep for several weeks.

Before serving, drain and slice the cabbage thinly, arrange in a salad bowl, sprinkle with paprika and olive oil and serve as an accompaniment to the meatballs (p. 72) or tas kebab (p. 62) or any roast or grilled meat.

Pickled Cabbage-Stuffed Green Peppers (Trushi di Pipiritzas Inchidas con Kol)

This two-in-one pickle may be unfamiliar but is well worth getting to know, especially with shishlik, kebab or grilled steak.

large-mouthed glass jar or crock large enough to hold the stuffed peppers or 2 smaller jars	⅓ cup salt
	5 stalks dill
	5 kernels allspice
12 small green peppers	10 peppercorns
1 small cabbage, shredded	6 cups water
2 carrots, diced	¼ cup plain white vinegar
2 stalks celery, with leaves, chopped	

Wash the peppers, cut off their crowns and remove all seeds without breaking the peppers.

In a large mixing bowl, mix together the cabbage, carrots and half the chopped celery. Sprinkle over 1½ tablespoons salt and rub it into the vegetables with the palms of your hands. Gently stuff the peppers with the vegetables. Cover the bottom of a wide-mouthed, large glass pickling jar with the remaining chopped celery and carefully begin to arrange the stuffed peppers upright in layers. Alternate the layers with sprigs of dill, the allspice and peppercorns, until the jar is filled.

Dissolve the remaining salt in the 6 cups water, add the vinegar and pour over the vegetables until covered. Top with sprigs of dill, tie a piece of cheesecloth over the mouth of the jar and store in a warm, light place until pickled, about 1 week.

When ready, discard the cheesecloth and cover with the original lid or foil. Store in cool dark place.

Pickled Cauliflower
(Trushi di Karfiol)

This easy-to-prepare pickle makes a lovely addition to the table and can be served also with cocktails. Simply drain the flowerettes and fill up a glass bowl.

wide-mouthed glass jar or crock, big enough to hold the cauliflower flowerettes	dill
	5 kernels allspice
	10 peppercorns
1 large cauliflower head, fresh and white	⅓ cup salt
	6 cups water
3 carrots, sliced diagonally	1 teaspoon plain vinegar
3 celery stalks, chopped coarsely, leaves separate	

Wash and separate the cauliflower into flowerettes. Cover the bottom of large, wide-mouthed glass jar with celery leaves. Add the cauliflower flowerettes alternating with carrots, celery and dill. Add the allspice and peppercorns.

Dissolve the salt in the water. Add the vinegar and pour over vegetables in the jar. Cover the jar opening with a piece of cheesecloth and store in a warm, light place for 4–6 days. Store in a cool dark place.

Pickled Watermelon
(Trushi di Carpus)

I believe that pickled watermelon is not unknown in the United States. This recipe makes a sweetish relish that titillates the tongue like a glass of champagne. For just the right taste, the watermelon should be nice and sweet.

1 smallish watermelon	1½ ounces salt (⅓ cup)
1 bunch celery with leaves, chopped	fresh dill sprigs
4 cups water	as many pickling jars as necessary
allspice kernels	

Cut the watermelon into slices about 2 inches thick and remove the outer rind, leaving the white inner rind intact. Discard the outer rinds, and again slice the watermelon into wedges of an inch thickness, retaining some white rind on each strip, and removing as many pips as possible without breaking up the watermelon. The number of pickling jars will depend upon the size of your watermelon. Cover the bottom of each jar with chopped celery for about 1 inch. Gently put in the watermelon wedges, alternating with chopped celery and 3 or 4 allspice kernels in each jar.

Dissolve the salt into the water, and pour over watermelon until covered. Top each jar with a few sprigs of dill, tie over a piece of cheesecloth and store in a warm, bright place for about a week until pickled. Remove the cheese-cloth, replace original lids, and store in cool, dark place.

Pickled Cucumbers
(Trushi di Pipinos)

Dill pickles — cucumbers, that is — can be made with or without vinegar. In this recipe the vinegar adds crunchiness and longevity.

1 large glass pickling jar	4–5 sprigs dill, whole
2 pounds small firm cucumbers	¼ cup salt
celery stalks and their leaves	4 cups water
6–10 cloves garlic, peeled	1 tablespoon white plain vinegar
6–10 peppercorns	

Wash and cut the tips from the cucumbers. Stuff a few of the celery stalks into the bottom of a wide-mouthed, large glass pickling jar. Arrange the cucumbers over, in horizontal layers or upright, alternating with garlic cloves and peppercorns. Put dill on top.

Dissolve the salt in the water, add the vinegar and pour over the cucumbers. Tie a cheesecloth over the opening of the jar and store in a bright place overnight. Next day, pour out the water into a bowl, taste for salt — it should be fairly salty; add salt or water as it calls for, and pour back into the jar. Let stand in a bright place until pickled, about a week, remove the cheesecloth and replace with original lid. Store in cool, dark place.

Pickled Half-Ripe Tomatoes
(Trushi di Domates Korelados)

If you have a garden of your own, this is a perfect way to take care of some of your surplus tomatoes. Pick them small and green, and use them whole rather than in quarters.

2 pounds still-somewhat-green tomatoes	10 garlic cloves, peeled
	2 carrots, thinly sliced
2 celery stalks, with leaves	¼ cup salt
dill	4 cups water

Wash the tomatoes. If they are very small, leave them whole. Stuff some of the celery stalks and sprigs of dill onto the bottom of a large, wide-mouthed glass pickling jar, and arrange the tomatoes in layers, alternating with garlic cloves and the carrots. Top with more celery and dill.

Dissolve the salt into the water and pour over the tomatoes in the jar. Tie a piece of cheesecloth over the top of the jar, and store in a bright place for about a week until pickled. When pickled, remove cheesecloth, replace original lid and store in cool, dark place.

SWEETS

Jean david

Sweets

Although heavy cakes were never served for dessert, and our full and substantial meals generally ended with fresh fruit or a light compote, there was no lack of sweets in our diet or occasion to eat them.

Most often sweets were reserved for a late afternoon pickup or to enjoy with guests, whenever they came, as a sign of hospitality, giving and well-being. On summer afternoons, a generous spoonful of *dolce blanco*, a soft caramel confection filled with toasted slivered almonds, might be served in a glass of cold water for an after-siesta refreshment. In winter, we children came home to a slice of buttered bread thickly spread with rich plum marmalade.

Visitors could expect the little cups of strong black coffee with which they were received to be accompanied by one or more confections. Inevitably, jelly, confiture or marmalade was brought out in little glass dishes and duly sampled with polished silver teaspoons that tinkled like small bells whenever they touched our plates. And some sort of cake, pie, pastry or halvah was usually on hand as well.

For special festivities such as births, weddings, briths and bar mitzvahs, almond cookies were prepared. And our milk-stewed rice, a sort of stove-top rice pudding, was sometimes eaten as a light meal.

With the exception of the pies and some of the cooked fruit dishes, our confections tend to be quite heavy and very sweet. Nuts, either as the major ingredient or as a generous filler for *fila* or other dough, are a frequent component and, as if that isn't enough, many of our cakes are thoroughly doused in a thick sugar syrup. Portions were small, but nobody complained.

I have selected for this chapter what might be considered representative samples of various groups of confections. There are the famous nut cookies and cakes and the nut-filled pastries of which *baklava* is the best known but of which many other types abound. There are recipes for fresh fruit pies and milk pies, for two types of halvah and for custard. Lastly, there are various types of fruit confections, ranging from baked quince to orange peel confiture, and a confiture of rose petals as well. Many of these, especially the halvahs and jams, can easily be bought today, but there is little resemblance between the store-bought variety and the home-made versions.

This is a plentiful array, and within each group further variations may readily be created. Almonds and walnuts are practically interchangeable, and pistachio nuts may be used as well. One type of fresh fruit may be exchanged for another in the pies, and the same holds true of the jams, where apples can be used instead of quince, lemon or grapfruit peel in place of orange peel, and dried apricots for black prunes.

Unbaked Almond Cookies
(Masapan)

Masapan — marzipan in English — was the sweet traditionally served at births, briths, weddings and bar mitzvahs, so when we saw the preparation in the kitchen we knew that a celebration was in tow. The soft almond confection comes straight from Spain, but ours has a more granular texture and, I would add, a more natural appearance: round and topped with a single blanched almond. The ones I recently ate in Spain, and which are also sold in Israel, come in a variety of fruit and flower shapes and are colored accordingly, which perhaps improves their looks but does nothing for their taste.

6½ cups shelled almonds (about 2 pounds)	juice of ½ lemon
4½ cups sugar	1 cup rose water
4 cups water	60 paper manchettes (serving cups)

If the almonds still have skins, blanch them for 1 minute in boiling water. This enables you to easily slip off the skins. Dry them well and set aside 30 for decoration. Grind the rest finely.

In a heavy saucepan bring the sugar and water to a boil. Skim the top and continue to boil, stirring occasionally with a wooden spoon, until the sugar reaches the soft ball stage (236°). Add the almonds and lemon juice to the sugar mixture and continue to cook for 2–3 minutes, stirring vigorously all the while. Remove from heat and continue to work the mixture until the mass no longer adheres to the sides of the pan. Allow to cool. Moisten your hands with rose water and form little ½-inch balls from the dough. Place them in paper manchettes and add ½ almond from those reserved for decoration on top. This is the traditional sweet served on festive occasions.

Makes 60 balls.

Baked Almond Cookies
(Marachunos)

These *marachunos* are a baked version of marzipan, with the egg whites considerably lightening the texture of the heavy almond paste. They are chewy cookies, which I never miss an occasion to serve. Some of my guests ask "What are they?" but once they bite, they realize they've tasted a very refined and moist almond macaroon.

3½ cups shelled almonds (1 pound) 2 cups sugar	whites of 2 eggs, lightly beaten to a foam 30 paper manchettes

Blanch the almonds for a minute in boiling water. Slip off their skins and dry. Reserve 15 for decoration; grind the remainder, not too finely. In a large bowl, mix together the almond and sugar. Fold in the egg whites, reserving about a teaspoon.

Moisten your hands with the reserved egg white and from the mixture form little balls, smoothing them by rolling them between your palms. Arrange the balls on a buttered baking dish. Top each with ½ almond from those reserved for decoration and bake in a 375° oven until firm and light golden, about 30 minutes. Place in paper manchettes to serve.

Makes 30 cookies.

Baklava with Almonds
(Baklava di Almendra)

Our version of the Mideastern baklava is made with almonds instead of the customary walnuts or pistachios, and bathed in sugar syrup instead of honey. Baking with fila dough may be new to you, but if you read the receipe before embarking, you'll realize that it's not at all forbidding.

2¾ cups shelled almonds	**The Syrup:**
¾ cup butter	2 cups sugar
½ cup light vegetable oil	1 cup water
1 pound fila leaves (12 inch by 12 inch sheets)	juice of ½ lemon
	¼ cup rose or orange water
12-inch square cake pan	

If the almonds still have their peels, blanch them for a minute in boiling water. Drain and slip off the peels. Allow them to dry and grind coarsely.

In a small saucepan melt the butter and oil together. Remove from heat. Brush the bottom of the baking pan with some of the mixture and spread a layer of fila sheet over the bottom. Brush the entire sheet with the butter-oil mixture and lay a second sheet over the first. Oil again and repeat with a third sheet. Brush the third sheet with the butter-oil and spread a layer of almonds across. Spread another two sheets of fila dough over, oiling each one in its turn. Atop the second layer spread another layer of almonds. Then another two layers of oiled fila dough. Continue in this way until the almonds are finished, and end with two sheets of oiled fila dough.

Tuck in the top sheets of fila dough around the sides of the lower layers so that it all looks like a well-made feather bed. Brush the top with the remaining butter-oil mixture. With a sharp knife slice through the baklava to the bottom in a criss-cross manner, creating little diamond-shaped cakes. Bake in a 350° oven until golden and crisp. Remove from oven and allow to cool. While the baklava is cooling, prepare the syrup.

The Syrup:
In a small saucepan bring the sugar and water to a boil and cook for about 5 minutes, until the water is slightly syrupy. Add the lemon juice and the rose or orange water and bring again to the boil. While the liquid is still hot, pour over the cooled baklava. Allow to stand for at least three hours before serving.

Nut-Filled Pastry
(Frigalda di Muez)

Thou similar to the more familiar baklava, this pastry is quite out of the ordinary. It's made by rolling up the nut-filled fila into pipes, which are then arranged in a coil starting from the outside of a round baking tin and moving inward. The overall visual effect is that of a snail. Since I think it's important to serve this special cake in a dish that complements its mood, I bake and bring it to the table in an attractive copper cake pan.

¾ cup butter	**The Syrup:**
3 tablespoons light vegetable oil	2 cups sugar
8 fila leaves	1 cup water
2 cups chopped walnuts	juice of ½ lemon
12-inch round baking tin	grated peel of 1 lemon
	(the lemon peel in the syrup can be replaced by ¼ cup rose water or orange water)

In a small saucepan, melt the butter into the oil.

Lay a clean linen towel atop a working surface and spread out one fila leaf across it. Brush the sheet with some of the oil-butter mixture and spread another fila leaf over. Brush again and spread ½ cup chopped walnuts over the pastry.

Roll up the pastry lengthwise, lightly and carefully lay the roll around the edge of the round baking tin. With another 2 fila leaves and another ½ cup walnuts, repeat the entire process, roll up and place in continuation to the first roll, working the roll around toward the center. Repeat the process twice more, by which time you should have a snail-shaped pastry filling the baking tin.

Brush the pastry with the remaining butter and oil and bake in a 350° oven until light golden and crisp, about 40 minutes. Allow to cool.

The Syrup:
Bring the water and sugar to a boil and allow to simmer for 6–8 minutes. Add lemon juice and lemon peel (or rose or orange water). While the syrup is still hot, prick the pastry all over and pour the syrup over it. Allow to sit for several hours before serving.

Almond Flour Cakes
(Tishpishti)

Sweet and heavy, these almond cakes are a cross between cookies and a rich butter cake. Except by the heartiest sweet lover, they can be eaten only in small portions.

¾ cup shelled almonds, slivered
6 cups flour
1 cup water
1 cup oil
½ cup butter, melted
12-inch square baking pan
20 almond halves for decoration

The Syrup:
3½ cups sugar
2½ cups water
1 vanilla pod
juice of ½ lemon

If the almonds still have peels, blanch them for a minute in boiling water, drain and slip off the skins. Sliver them into lengthwise strips. Mix the almond slivers well with the flour.

In a pan large enough to hold the flour-almond mixture as well, bring the water, oil and butter to a boil. Quickly add the flour-almond mixture, mix well and remove from heat.

Spread the mixture evenly into the baking pan. With a sharp knife, criss-cross the batter making diamond-shaped cakes. Place half an almond on each diamond shape. Bake in a hot oven, 375°, for 15 minutes. Lower the heat to 325° and bake until light golden, another 25 minutes. Allow to cool.

The Syrup:
In a saucepan bring the sugar, water and vanilla pod to a boil. Add the lemon juice and cook for 4 minuts. Remove from heat, and while still hot pour the mixture over the cooled *tishpishti.*

Kadaif

Kadaif are extremely thin noodles, shaped like flattened vermicelli, and are available fresh in Mideastern specialty shops. While baklava is the most familiar Mideastern sweet, this is no less typical. Be sure to serve it only after all the sugar syrup has thoroughly soaked into the cake.

2 cups coarsely chopped walnuts	**The Syrup:**
¼ cup sugar	3 cups sugar
grated peel of 1 lemon	3 cups water
1 pound *kadaif*	juice of ½ lemon
¾ cup melted butter	
12-inch square baking tin	

In a mixing bowl mix the coarsely chopped walnuts with the sugar and lemon peel.

Butter the baking dish and spread half of the uncooked *kadaif* across the bottom. Drip half of the melted butter over the *kadaif* and over that spread the walnut mixture. Cover with the rest of the *kadaif* and drip the remaining butter over the top. With a sharp knife, criss-cross incisions into diamond shapes. Bake in a 350° oven until golden and crisp, about 40 minutes. Allow to cool.

The Syrup:
In a saucepan bring the sugar and water to a boil. Cook for 5–6 minutes. Add lemon juice and remove from heat. Pour the syrup over the cooled *kadaif.* Cover with a towel to prevent drying and allow to rest for a few hours.

Walnut-Filled Crescents
(Roscas di Alhashu)

These nut-filled crescents are our traditional Purim sweet. Their shape is actually meant to suggest Haman's ears, though I don't know why.

6 tablespoons milk	1½ cups sugar
½ cup sugar	grated rind of 1 lemon
1 egg, lightly beaten	8 tablespoons milk
¾ cup margarine	
1 pound cake flour	**Topping:**
2 teaspoons baking powder	lightly beaten egg
	handful sesame seeds (available in
Filling:	supermarkets and Mideastern
2½ cups ground walnuts	specialty stores)

In a small saucepan heat the milk and sugar until the sugar dissolves. Remove from fire. Add the lightly beaten egg and the margarine and mix well until the margarine dissolves.

Sift the flour and baking powder onto a work surface and make a well in the center. Pour in the milk-margarine mixture and work lightly with the tips of your fingers until the texture is that of a light dough. Form a ball, place in a plastic bag and chill in the refrigerator for at least an hour.

When ready to prepare, mix the ground nuts, sugar and lemon rind. Bind together with the milk.

Divide the dough into six small balls. On a floured board, roll out one ball into a circle ¼-inch thick. Slice the dough, pie-like, into eight triangles.

Place a teaspoon of filling onto the larger end of each triangle and roll up each one into a crescent shape, rounding them at the end. Repeat the process with each of the six balls.

Brush the crescents with lightly beaten egg and dust with sesame seeds. Arrange on buttered baking sheet and bake in a 400° oven until golden, about 15–20 minutes.

Makes about 48 crescents.

Milk Custard
(Leche Papeada)

This custard has the consistency of a thick and rich cream, using as it does, no eggs at all. Milk custards date back to antiquity, when they were baked in shallow earthenware pans. Back home, we used a large, low-walled copper dish called a *tipsi*. But for this recipe I have substituted the more available pot-de-creme or souffle dish.

2 cups milk	**Caramel:**
2 teaspoons flour	3 tablespoons sugar
1 cup sweet cream	8 individual pot-de-creme or
1½ cups sugar	souffle dishes
vanilla pod, split, or	
1 teaspoon vanilla	

In a mixing bowl dissolve the flour in a little of the milk. Add the remaining milk to the mixture. Add the cream, the sugar and vanilla.

In a small saucepan over a medium heat, heat the 3 tablespoons of sugar. When it is melted to a golden color, pour a bit into each pot-de-creme or souffle dish. Tilt around to cover the bottom and cool until the sugar hardens.

Gently pour the milk mixture into each dish, filling each about ¾ full. Arrange the little dishes in a very shallow pan of water and bake uncovered in a slow (300°) oven for 45 minutes or until set and a crust has been formed. Serve chilled.

Serves 8.

Apricot Pie
(Inchusa di Apricos)

This pie uses a particularly light and crumbly dough. If you have trouble spreading it with your fingers, place it in a plastic bag, roll it out with a rolling pin, then peel off the bag and place the crust in position. I hope that you aren't tempted to substitute canned apricots for the fresh ones, as there is really no comparison in the freshness or subtlety of the taste.

Dough:	Filling:
2½ cups flour	2½ pounds fresh apricots, pitted and halved
3 tablespoons vanilla sugar	
rind of 1 lemon, grated	¾ cup sugar
½ teaspoon salt	1 tablespoon cornstarch
1 cup margarine, softened to room temperature	granulated and powdered sugar for dusting
1 egg yolk	12-inch pie tin

Place the flour on a working surface, sprinkle over the vanilla sugar, grated rind and salt. Form a well and place softened margarine and egg yolk in the middle. With the tips of your fingers incorporate quickly the flour into the margarine-egg mixture. Form a ball, cut in quarters and reassemble the parts into another ball. Repeat the process, cutting the ball and reforming, twice more, place in a plastic bag and let rest in the refrigerator for an hour.

Filling:
Put the apricot halves with the sugar in a heavy saucepan over a low heat and cook until sugar melts. Dissolve the cornstarch in a little bit of cold water and add to the apricots. Continue cooking until the mixture thickens.

In a buttered 12-inch pie tin spread half of the dough. Sprinkle a tablespoon of granulated sugar over it. Add the apricot mixture and spread the second half of the dough over the top.

Seal the pie by pinching edges together and prick the top with a fork. Bake in a 350° oven for 45–55 minutes. The dough will be crisp but still pale. Before serving dust with powdered sugar.

Grape Tartlets
(Kazadas di Ouva)

There was a time when these little tartlets were fashioned by hand, and on completion every single one of the batch looked as though they had come out of the same machine. Today, of course, we expect no such wonders and I suggest molding them in muffin or individual pastry tins. They look magnificent on a dessert tray, where they mix well with other cakes and cookies.

Dough:	Filling:
2½ cups flour	1 egg white, lightly beaten
2 tablespoons vanilla sugar	1–2 pounds seedless grapes
rind of 1 lemon, grated	sugar
½ teaspoon salt	powdered sugar for dusting
1 cup margarine	2 muffin tins of twelve muffin
1–2 tablespoons ice water	molds each

Sift the flour into a bowl, add the vanilla sugar, lemon rind, salt and the margarine, cut into small pieces. In a food mixer or with a pastry cutter or two small knives, cut the margarine into the flour until the pastry has the consistency of coarse cornmeal. Add 1 or 2 tablespoons ice water. Quickly form into a ball and put into a plastic bag. Store in the refrigerator for at least one hour.

Divide the dough in half and place one half in the refrigerator. Roll out the remaining half on a floured surface until ¼ inch thick. With a glass or cookie cutter cut circles large enough to fit each muffin mold with some overlap. Line the tins with the dough and brush the insides with lightly beaten egg white. Put in the refrigerator to chill for an hour.

Fill each section to the brim with grapes and sprinkle 1 teaspon sugar over each tart.

Roll out the remaining dough and cut out similar circles. Cover each tartlet with a dough circle and pinch the edges together. Bake in a preheated 350° oven for about 30 minutes or until golden.

Remove each tartlet by running a sharp knife around the edge. Before serving, dust with powdered sugar.

Makes 24.

Sour Cherry Pie
(Inchusa di Vishna)

The cherry traditionally used in this pie was the brightly colored, slightly tart *amarena* — amarelle or marachino — that enjoys a short season in the late spring. If you want to keep them for future pies, cook the cherries together with the sugar for a few minutes, cool, and place in the freezer until ready for use.

2½ cups flour	**Filling:**
3 tablespoons vanilla sugar	2½ pounds fresh sour cherries
½ teaspoon salt	*(amarenas)*, pitted
1 cup margarine or butter, softened	1 cup sugar
to room temperature	powdered sugar for dusting
1 egg, separated (yolk for crust,	
white for filling)	12-inch pie tin

Place 2½ cups flour on board, sprinkle the vanilla sugar and salt on top. Form a well and place softened margarine and egg yolk in the middle. Working quickly with the tips of your fingers, incorporate the flour into the margarine-egg mixture.

Form a ball, cut in quarters, reassemble the parts into another ball and repeat the process twice more. Place the ball in a plastic bag and allow to rest in the refrigerator for an hour.

Wash the cherries and remove the stems and pits. Put in a colander, add ¼ cup of the sugar and allow to drain for 1 hour.

Roll out half of the dough to a ¼ inch thickness and fit into the buttered 12-inch pie tin. Brush the inside with the beaten egg white and bake in a moderate oven for 15 minutes.

Remove from oven, and pour the drained cherries into the pan. Sprinkle the remaining ¾ cup sugar over them. Roll out the remaining half of the dough and cover the pie.

Seal the pie by pinching the edges, prick the top all over with a fork and bake in a preheated 350° oven, about 45–55 minutes.

When cool, sprinkle with powdered sugar and serve.

Milk Pie (1)
(Inchusa di Leche)

The following two milk pies are versions of the creamy, custard-like tarts that were so often served at our tea table. Both are ancient recipes that have undoubtably gone through many adaptations. The first, you will notice, is for an uncovered pie.

2 cups flour	**Filling:**
3 tablespoons vanilla sugar	4 cups milk
½ teaspoon salt	1 vanilla pod, split
rind of 1 lemon, grated	8 tablespoons sugar
½ cup margarine or butter, softened to room temperature	8 egg yolks beaten until light yellow
⅓ cup light vegetable oil	12-inch round pie pan
⅓ cup milk	

Sift the 2 cups flour onto a board, sprinkle the vanilla sugar, salt and the lemon rind over. Form a well and put the softened margarine (or butter) in the center. Add the oil and milk and with the tips of your fingers quickly incorporate the flour into the center mixture. Without kneading, form a ball, place in a plastic bag and allow to rest in the refrigerator for at least an hour.

Filling:
In a large pan, heat the milk, vanilla pod and sugar until the sugar melts. Remove from heat. Add the beaten egg yolks slowly, stirring the mixture all the while.

Lightly butter the pie pan. Roll out the dough and spread in pie pan. Prick all over with a fork and pour in the milk-egg mixture. Bake in a 350° oven until the mixture sets and turns golden, about 45 minutes.

Milk Pie (2)
(Inchusa di Leche)

Browsing through a Spanish cookbook, I found almost the identical recipe. Unlike the previous pie, this one is covered and has a caramel, flan-like quality.

Dough:	Vanilla Cream:
3 cups flour	4 egg yolks
3 tablespoons vanilla sugar	2 cups milk
½ teaspoon salt	1 teaspoon cornstarch
1 lemon rind, grated	¾ cup sugar
1 cup margarine or butter,	vanilla pod, split
softened to room temperature	1 lemon rind, grated
1 whole egg	¼ cup butter
	10-inch round pie tin

The Dough:

Heap the flour on a clean work surface and sprinkle the vanilla sugar, salt and lemon rind over it. Form a well in the middle and drop in the softened margarine and egg. With the tips of your fingers incorporate the flour quickly into the margarine-egg mixture.

Form a ball, cut in quarters, place one quarter on top of another and work again into a ball. Repeat the process twice more, put in a plastic bag and let rest in the refrigerator for at least an hour.

Vanilla Cream:

In a heavy saucepan, beat the egg yolks lightly. Dissolve the cornstarch in the milk and add to the egg yolks. Add the sugar, vanilla and lemon rind and put over a low heat whisking it all the time. Just as the mixture begins to bubble, remove from the heat and continuing to whisk, add the butter bit by bit. Cover and allow to cool.

To assemble: Roll out half of the dough into a round large enough to line the pie tin and prick with a fork all over. Pour in the milk mixture. Roll out the second half of the dough to cover the pie. Pinch the edges together, brush with egg yolk, score the top with a fork and bake in a preheated 350° oven until light golden, about 40–45 minutes.

Milk-Stewed Rice
(Leche con Aroz)

A close relative of baked rice pudding, this dessert is made quite simply by cooking rice in milk flavored with vanilla and adding sugar, plenty of lemon rind, cream and cinnamon in the appropriate order. Use a large lemon as this is what gives the dish its special perk.

¾ cup rice	½ teaspoon salt
4 cups milk	rind of 1 lemon, grated
vanilla pod, split	½ cup sweet cream
¾ cup sugar	1 teaspoon cinnamon

Put the rice, the milk and vanilla pod over a slow heat to cook. When the rice is almost tender, add the sugar, salt and grated lemon rind. Continue cooking until the rice has absorbed all the milk. Remove from heat, remove the vanilla pod and add the sweet cream. Mix well and pour into a glass bowl. Sprinkle with ground cinnamon. Serve cold.

Serves 6.

Semolina Halvah
(Halvah di Gris)

Halvah, as it is known to Americans, is a confection of sesame paste and honey. But it can take many forms, including this version made with semolina and almonds. It is a light and grainy confection.

1 cup almonds, peeled and sliced	1 cup sugar
½ cup butter	vanilla pod
1 cup semolina (cream of wheat)	1 teaspoon cinnamon
	wax paper
Syrup:	almond halves for decorating
2 cups water	

If the almonds still have their peels, drop them into boiling water for a minute and slip off the skins. Slice.

Prepare the semolina. In a heavy saucepan large enough to hold both the semolina and the three cups of syrup, melt the butter and add the semolina and almond slices. Cook over a low heat until the butter is absorbed.

The syrup: In another saucepan, bring the water, sugar and vanilla pod to a boil. Continue to cook only until the sugar is completely dissolved, and pour the mixture over the semolina.

Return the semolina to the heat, and cook slowly, for 15 minutes, mixing all the while. Add the cinnamon and mix again. Remove from heat, cover and allow to rest for one hour.

Spread the mixture on a large piece of wax paper into a rectangle of about 1 inch thickness. Cut into small 1½ inch squares and top each square with half an almond.

Baked Quince
(Bimbrijos al Orno)

Though rare in the U.S., quince is worth looking for. Uncooked, this is a hard, inedible fruit, which, inidentally, we children used to stick full of cloves and carry to synagogue on Yom Kippur to keep us from fainting. Properly prepared, it makes a lovely, slightly tart dessert. Here is a recipe for baked quince, an interesting alternative to the well-known baked apple, that has the further advantage of giving off a most glorious jelly that can be eaten as is with a spoon or on a slice of buttered toast.

6 large quinces	8–10 tablespoons sugar
juice of one lemon in a large bowl of water	1 cup water
	whipped cream (optional)

Wash and rub the quinces with a cloth to remove its fuzzy down. Cut each in half, top to bottom, remove the core and pips and drop into a bowl of water to which has been added the juice of one lemon. When all have been cored, arrange the quince halves, skin side down in a baking dish. Sprinkle half the sugar evenly over all the quinces, add ½ cup water on the bottom and bake in a hot 375° oven for twenty minutes.

Remove from oven, turn the quinces over, add the rest of the sugar and water and bake for another 20 minutes. Serve with whipped cream if you like. When cool the syrup turns into a jelly.

Serves 12.

Quince and Sour Apple Paste
(Pasta di Bimbrijo)

A chewy, tart and tangy confection that was kept as far as possible from the reach of children. It was made at the beginning of the winter, when the quince and the apple came into season, and kept in tin containers. As it aged, the taste and aroma thickened and intensified.

2 pounds quince	½ cup water
3 sour apples	sugar for dusting
1 pound sugar (2¼ cups)	

Wash the quince and remove the fuzzy down. Cut into quarters, core and pit. Core and pit the sour apples, and place all the fruit in a larg enamel or pyrex saucepan with water to cover. Cook until the fruit is soft, drain and blend in a food processor, or pass through a sieve.

Wash out the saucepan and put in the sugar and water. Bring to a boil and cook until the sugar reaches the brittle stage, about 300°. Add the fruit pulp, mix well and continue to cook until the mixture, when dropped from a spoon, keep its shape.

Oil a large platter or rectangle of wax paper and spread the paste to about 1 to 1½ inches thickness. With a sharp knife cut into squares, cover with a clean cloth or cheesecloth, and allow to dry. The drying process takes at least a day.

When the paste squares are dry, roll each in sugar and store in a covered glass jar or tin box.

White Sweet
(Dulci Blanco)

This creamy confection can be eaten spread on bread or as we used to eat it — a spoonful suspended in a glass of very cold water. It is delightfully refreshing after a siesta on a summer afternoon.

5½ cups sugar	1 cup almonds, slivered and toasted
2½ cups water	to light brown
	grated peel of 1 lemon

In a large enamel or pyrex saucepan bring the sugar and water to a boil. Continue cooking until the soft ball stage (236°) is reached.

Remove from heat and beat with a wooden spoon until the mixture turns milky, at least several minutes. Add the almonds and lemon peel and spoon into a covered glass jar for storage.

Rose-Petal Confiture
(Dulci di Rozas)

Bulgaria's famous Valley of the Roses scents the surrounding air for miles and miles. The essence of roses is used as the base of the most prestigious perfumes in the world. And from the petals of the lovely pink roses, we make a confiture that preserves the aroma intact through the steps of preparation and storage right to the table itself.

9 ounces rose petals	2½ pounds sugar
½ teaspon lemon salt	1 teaspoon lemon juice
4 cups water	

Rub half the rose petals with lemon salt. They will change color and become darker. Put the remaining half into a saucepan with 4 cups water and boil for 5 minutes. Allow to cool and then strain, reserving both water and rose petals.

Measure out 3 cups of the water in which the rose petals have cooked. Put into a large saucepan with all the rose petals, the sugar and the lemon juice. Bring to a boil, lower the heat and cook slowly for 15 minutes. Increase the heat and boil for another 15 minutes.

Do not stir but shake the pan from time to time. When the syrup reaches the soft ball stage (236°) remove from heat. Allow to cool slightly and store in hermetically sealed glass jars.

Orange Peel Confiture
(Aniikos di Portokal)

This recipe describes the way my grandmother made these delicious little candies — by coiling the strips of orange peel and stringing them along a thread. But the candies taste every bit as good if you simply blanch and boil the skins in the sugar syrup after they are grated. My grandmother's method produces very pretty little confections; the simpler procedure saves time and sugar-sticky fingers.

peels of 6 large eating oranges	2 cups water
2 pounds sugar	

Choose oranges with thick skins. Peel the oranges, removing from the peel as much of the thick white pith as possible. Cut the peel into strips. Roll each strip into a ring resembling a snail and string them along a thread (easily done with a darning needle). Tie the ends of the thread to prevent the orange peel slipping off. Blanch the string of peels in boiling water and let drain.

In an enamel or pyrex pan bring the sugar and the water to a boil. Let boil for a few minutes. Immerse the strings of orange peel strips into the boiling syrup and let boil until the syrup reaches the soft ball stage (236°). Remove from heat. Let cool and, with a little bit of luck, you will be able to remove the strings. Store in glass jars.

Prune Marmalade
(Marmalada di Prunas Negras)

These prune preserves are made by long baking rather than the convention-al boiling. We always prepared them in enormous quantities — enough to get us through the long winters, when they were a staple for breakfast and in the afternoons on buttered bread for children. This recipe, of course, is for a relatively small amount.

2 pounds black prunes, pitted	3 cinnamon sticks
1½ pounds sugar (approx. 3½ cups)	5 cloves
	3 tablespoons wine vinegar

Wash the prunes and remove the pits. Arrange in a baking dish cut side up, cover with sugar, add cinnamon and cloves around them. Sprinkle the vinegar evenly across the top and bake in a 375° oven for 1½ hours. Remove from oven and allow to cool. Spoon into glass jars for storage.

INDEX

224

227